PROFITPRENEURSHIP

Creating a Business that Produces
Outstanding Financial Results

Ren J. Carlton, CPA, CSMC

Results
Matter!

ISBN: 1439261210
ISBN-13: 9781439261217

DEDICATION

This book is dedicated to my beautiful wife Karen
and my wonderful children Sara and Ryan.

TABLE OF CONTENTS

FOREWORD

I was introduced to Ren Carlton by sheer accident. While working in my office on a Saturday morning, I was scanning the AM radio dial and came across someone talking about business in a talk show format. I was intrigued by the host of the Business Reality Network, so I turned up the volume, stopped what I was doing, and sat back to listen. The host had some very unique perspectives on how entrepreneurs need to view and manage their businesses in order to satisfy their need for profit as it relates to their long-term goal of success. After the show, I e-mailed the host and suggested a couple of questions he might want to address in a subsequent show. He called me within a half hour and invited me to be a guest. Over the next three years, I was a guest on the Business Reality Network a half dozen times. Each time, Ren and I would engage in an in-depth conversation about topics related to business creation, business development, and the various scenarios that surround these exciting subjects.

Ren takes the position that the accounting profession is similar to the study of history and the finance profession is a look into the future. I thought this was a very unique way to approach these subjects, and I've often used these comparisons when lecturing entrepreneurs and small business owners on why they need to differentiate between their accountants and their business financial advisors. On his radio show, Ren routinely engaged in in-depth discussions with a variety of entrepreneurs on very important subjects pertaining to running small, medium, and large companies.

This book allows Ren to re-visit many of these important subjects to talk about why profit is such an important driver in a successful business. He discusses the need for businesses to set budgets and hold everyone in the company accountable for maintaining them. Planning, execution, and accountability are three areas that are successfully targeted in this book. In order for a business to present itself well and carry itself properly, all areas of the financial framework need to be addressed. This book details all aspects of analyzing and utilizing the various financial steps that are required to carry on a successful business venture. Without a sound financial base and a firm understanding of how financial infrastructure keeps a business afloat, entrepreneurs are doomed to fail. The succeeding chapters detail what entrepreneurs need to know, what professional support they need to engage, and what results they should expect to obtain.

With my background as both a business coach and entrepreneur, I understand that successful businesses must produce profits. Profit is the engine that drives business. It has been my privilege to meet Ren, be a guest on his radio show, and discuss this subject in a variety of forums. As a business person, you will learn a great deal from and be entertained by reading *Profitpreneurship.*

Ron Cocquyt
President, Hylander Management LLC, Professional Business Coaching Services. Formerly executive vice president, partner, and inventor for Monarch Products Inc. (Medical manufacturing company sold to Johnson & Johnson in 1992.)

PREFACE

I have been preaching Profitpreneurship in one form or another for the past ten years. Although the specific processes and techniques have evolved, my overall mission has remained the same. Help businesses, organizations, and individuals create outstanding financial results (cash and profits). My primary conduit for this message has always been my consulting firm, Dynamic Advisory Solutions. Although we have enjoyed sustained growth and success, we can only reach so many clients.

That is why I have always enjoyed public speaking. If you look at my website, www.rencarlton.com, you will see I speak to entrepreneurial groups any chance I get, both on a volunteer and compensated basis. It is a great way to reach entrepreneurs in need—even if they cannot afford my firm's services.

My award-winning radio program, Business Reality Network, was essentially public speaking on steroids! Not only did I reach thousands of listeners on a weekly basis, but the format also forced me to formalize my content and processes. This ultimately benefitted both my paying clients, as well as my entrepreneurial listening audience.

This book is yet another way for me to reach a broader audience. Formatting my content was difficult for the radio. It was brutal for this book. This task was by far one of the most difficult endeavors I have ever undertaken. That being said, it is also tremendously rewarding. I am now able to broadcast the Profitpreneurship message globally. Although this book obviously cannot compete with the value of one-on-one consulting, the readers of *Profitpreneurship* will receive a lot of the same value for a relatively low cost. I hope you enjoy my efforts.

ACKNOWLEDGEMENTS

I would not have been able to write this book without the help and support of numerous individuals. To my extremely supportive wife Karen, who proofread countless revisions of this book. To my children Sara and Ryan, who always put a smile on my face even after the most tedious of work days. To my family and friends, for giving me their constant love and support. A special thank you to Craig Gladden for his "final review." I would like to thank EO Detroit for being a great resource for ideas and encouragement. Thank you to all of my clients for trusting me and my firm with their businesses' well-being. And finally, a special thank you to my staff at Dynamic Advisory Solutions (DAS), for their help in achieving our firm's growth and profitability goals.

INTRODUCTION – CREATING A PROFIT-DRIVEN BUSINESS

"Entrepreneurs are simply those who understand that there is little difference between obstacle and opportunity and are able to turn both to their advantage." Niccolo Machiavelli

This book is about creating a business that makes money. Real money! Every business is a high-risk venture. Without a high rate of return, your business is a poor use of your capital. This book is dedicated to building processes and habits in order to produce outstanding financial results.

I am a management consultant with one true passion—making money. I am passionate about making money for myself, my clients, my radio listeners, and my readers. My financial and consulting skills allow me to help people create wealth through entrepreneurship. This book documents my firm's process for building profit-driven businesses.

This book was inspired by a seminar I developed entitled "Greed is Good, how to build a profit-driven business." I thought the title was clever, but others disagreed. Below is one of the e-mails I received in response to my seminar (I am assuming this individual did not attend):

"This is a poor choice for a seminar title, especially in this economy. I think a lot of people will not see the humor in it. Besides, greed is never good in business; both parties need to benefit."

This response resonated with me. After thinking about the above message, I must disagree with my detractor. The quest for resources is typically a zero-sum game. Two people can't wear the same pair of pants, eat the same meal, be president of the same company, etc. After thinking about the concept of greed further, I thought the definition of greed would offer clarity:

Greed is the selfish desire for or pursuit of money, wealth, power, food, or other possessions, especially when this denies the same

goods to others. It is generally considered a vice, and is one of the seven deadly sins in Catholicism. Source, Wikipedia

Well, I don't know about you, but I do not know many people who don't pursue money, wealth, power, and/or food. Maybe it is the denial of others that is the problem. But again, aren't we talking about a zero-sum game? If we have something, doesn't that deny someone else from having it? Maybe not…

"If one farmer is raising 2 percent more corn and hogs every year and his neighbor is raising 4 percent more, then they are eating more every year (or trading more away.) If this disparity goes on for a long time, one of them will become significantly richer than the other, which may become a source of envy or political friction, but they are both growing steadily better off. The important point is that productivity growth, like so much else in economics, is not a zero-sum game." Charles Wheelan, *Naked Economics*

I disagree with the unlimited wealth concept described in Wheelan's book. What the above scenario fails to acknowledge is what happens to the extra 2 percent of productivity. Assuming the farmer is going to sell the additional corn and hogs produced, won't that sale deprive another farmer from selling his goods? After all, there is a limited amount of demand for the supply. Speaking of the law of supply and demand, theoretically the additional supply of goods will also push down the overall price of corn and hogs (think China and Wal-Mart). The limited amount of consumers for any given product or service validates the zero-sum game philosophy.

Since our economy is a zero-sum game, my assertion is that greed is a necessary component of a successful business. Whether it is greed for growth, greed for better employees, or greed for success, greed is a requirement. It may not be politically correct, but it is the truth. THIS IS OK. Greed is good. But just like anything else, there can be too much of a good thing. Excess greed leads to problems.

"Cornell economist Robert Frank, author of Luxury Fever, *has made a persuasive case that relative wealth—the size of my pie compared to my neighbor's—is an important determinant of our utility. He offered survey respondents a choice between two worlds: (A): You earn $110,000 and everyone else earns $200,000. Or (B): You earn $100,000 and everyone else earns $85,000. As he explains, 'The income figures represent real purchasing power. Your income in World A would command a house 10 percent larger than you could afford in World B, 10 percent more restaurant dinners and so on. By choosing World B, you'd give up a small amount of absolute income in return for a large increase in relative income.' You would be richer in World A; you would be less wealthy in World B but richer than everyone else. Which scenario would make you happier? Mr. Frank found that a majority of Americans choose B. In other words, relative income does matter. Envy may be part of the explanation. It is also true, Mr. Frank points out, that in complex social environments we seek ways to evaluate our performance. Relative wealth is one of them."*
Charles Wheelan, *Naked Economics*

I think the above scenario illustrates the difference between greed and what I call Profitpreneurship. Profitpreneurship is not about driving value at the pointless expense of others. Profitpreneurship is not about relative wealth. Profitpreneurship is about building a business that maintains processes and habits necessary to drive financial success. Sure, this often requires depriving other businesses of income, market share, etc. However, Profitpreneurship is required to create and sustain long-term business success.

Who Should Read This Book

This book is designed for the following audiences:
1. Business owners interested in creating a business that produces outstanding financial results.
2. Family businesses looking to run their company like a business.
3. Business units, departments, and divisions interested in improving financial performance.

4. Financial and accounting professionals looking to improve their skills.
5. Wannabe entrepreneurs looking to start their own business the right way.
6. Non-profit organizations that want to sustain their presence in the community. This group includes churches, charities, hospitals, and schools.

How to Read This Book

This book takes you through the Dynamic Advisory Solutions (DAS) Profit Process. The DAS Profit Process is the method I use to help businesses achieve outstanding financial results. The DAS Profit Process has the following six components:
1. Transactional Accounting
2. Reporting
3. Powerful Budgets
4. Financing
5. Company Dashboards
6. Employees Scorecards

The focus of this book is implementing steps 3-6 of The DAS Profit Process. It is important to note that these steps must be implemented in sequential order. Financial statements are meaningless without accurate transactional accounting processes. It is impossible to implement our powerful budgeting process without timely and accurate financial statements. Since this book only covers steps 3-6 of The DAS Profit Process, you need to make sure your accounting department is properly performing your company's transactional accounting duties. In addition, you also need to make sure you have timely and accurate financial reporting. If these areas are not functioning properly, my consulting firm can help. The DAS Diagnostic identifies problems with your accounting department, especially with transactional accounting and management reporting, and provides a detailed time and action plan to resolve any issues (I apologize, but I am a shameless self-promoter).

Each chapter begins with one or two of my favorite quotes, followed by a listing of chapter highlights. Each chapter concludes with a list of action items. These are steps you should take to implement the concepts described in the chapter.

No Whining!

I do a lot of public speaking and consulting based on the principles of this book. At one of my presentations to entrepreneurs, there was a human resources specialist in the audience. After my discussion on maximizing employee performance (Chapter 4 of this book), he voiced his disagreement with my techniques. Some of his criticisms included:

1. You cannot measure employee performance strictly by numbers.
2. Your techniques will not motivate poor performers. All you will do is create an uncomfortable environment for them. This will ultimately cause them to quit.
3. You should not publically display employee performance metrics if they are tied to compensation.

I definitely respect his point and opinion, but the issues above are not relevant to my presentation (or this book). My techniques are not meant to motivate poorly performing employees to do their job. This book will not help you feel good about missing goals. Profitpreneurship is about taking a pragmatic approach to driving growth and profits for your business. At times this approach is extremely uncomfortable, especially to underperformers. That is OK. Poor performance should be uncomfortable. After all, isn't poor performance already uncomfortable for the business owner?

Don't get me wrong, I understand you cannot run a business strictly by the numbers. There are countless other books on the subject. I realize there is a time and a place for the warm and fuzzy stuff. However, that place is not in this book.

DISCLAIMER

Although all of the stories in this book are true, several small aspects of these stories have been altered in order to protect the identity (and feelings) of my clients and colleagues. To ensure compliance with U.S. Treasury Department regulations, we inform you that any tax advice that may be contained in this communication (including any attachments) is not intended or written to be used, and cannot be used, for purposes of (i) avoiding tax-related penalties under the Internal Revenue Code or applicable state or local tax law provisions or (ii) promoting, marketing, or recommending to another party any tax-related matters addressed herein.

CHAPTER 1: THE CASE FOR PROFITPRENEURSHIP – WHEN GREED IS GOOD

"...Greed, for lack of a better word, is good. Greed is right. Greed works. Greed clarifies, cuts through and captures the essence of the evolutionary spirit. Greed, in all of its forms—greed for life, for money, for love, knowledge—has marked the upward surge of mankind. And Greed, you mark my words, will not only save Teldar Paper but that other malfunctioning corporation called the USA." Gordon Gekko (Michael Douglas), *Wall Street*

"The problem of social organization is how to set up an arrangement under which greed will do the least harm; capitalism is that kind of a system." Milton Friedman

Chapter Highlights
1. Definition of Profitpreneurship
2. Why Profitpreneurship is critical to business success

I am blessed that most of my family lives close to me. Occasionally we play Monopoly. This is one of my favorite games. I enjoy the quest for acquiring assets, negotiating financial transactions, and accumulating wealth. What's not to like? I am very good at the game as long as everyone operates under one simple premise:

Everyone is greedy (e.g., trying to win and denying victory to others)

Based on this premise, I am extremely good at making trades and deals with competitors. One of my tactics is to make trades that will benefit an individual immediately, but will not give me an immediate benefit (e.g., give an individual one property that creates a monopoly in exchange for multiple "meaningless" properties). Eventually everyone will have a monopoly, and I will end up with the remaining "meaningless" properties. The trick is that when you combine all these meaningless properties, you often create multiple monopolies! This results in a substantial advantage over the other players.

I am a greedy Monopoly player.

Here is the flaw in my technique. My father does not play to win; he plays to play (which is a foreign concept to me). My entire tactic is based on the premise that everyone wants to win. Therefore, I offer too-good-to-be-true individual deals. He doesn't care. He wants to help give my mother/brother/sister-in-law a monopoly in exchange for nothing. He helps them out, in spite of setting himself up for disaster. He almost never wins. If a business owner ran her company like my father plays Monopoly, it wouldn't be long before her employees would be on the streets starving.

How do *you* play Monopoly?

Profitpreneurship

All businesses intend to be successful. Unfortunately, far fewer accomplish this goal. In order to enjoy both short- and long-term success, businesses need to produce profits and positive cash flow. Or to put it more simply, cash coming in needs to exceed cash going out. Businesses unable to do this will eventually fail.

Profitpreneurship is entrepreneurship with a twist. Profitpreneurship is the art of creating businesses that generate cash and profits on a consistent basis. Profitpreneurship is not simply the act of owning a business. It is the act of owning a business that produces outstanding financial results. Profitpreneurship is not about wanting to produce cash and profits. After all, who becomes a business owner with the goal of losing money? Profitpreneurship is actively building a business that maintains processes and habits necessary to drive financial success.

In order to illustrate the point, I will share a story about one of my clients. We were introduced to this particular client by a turnaround consultant. Their loans were being serviced by the special assets department of the bank. If you are unfamiliar with this department, consider yourself lucky. It is essentially where your loans go when the bank wants you to pay all your loans back... NOW! The turn-around consultant told the owners that they would be lucky if they kept their home after everything was liquidated.

Fortunately, the liquidation never happened. Over the course of four years, we were able to help them turn everything around. We helped them get out of the special assets department of the bank by convincing a different bank to take a chance with our client. Leveraging our reputation, we were able to secure a more traditional lending relationship. We were also able to help them get out of the dying automotive sector and into the red-hot aerospace industry. At the end of the four years, we helped them sell the business for an amount large enough so the owners would never have to work another day of their lives. During the process of selling their business, the owners were asked how they did it. Below is a paraphrased version of one of the owners' response:

"We started off being a sales-driven organization. Everything we did was focused on obtaining market share. We took on any work we could. Granted we did not totally ignore margins, but they definitely did not get the attention they deserved. As the bottom line continued to worsen, we continued to try and sell ourselves out of our problems. It simply didn't work. We were good at a lot of things, but we weren't great at anything. Every job had a major learning curve.

"Then we became an operations-based company. We focused on creating the highest quality products. We hired the best engineers. Our service was second to none. The only problem was our clients were unwilling to pay for the level of quality we were producing. We priced ourselves right out of the market.

"Finally we became profit-driven. We only sold jobs we knew we could make good money on. We managed our margins to the extreme. If we had a job lose money, we wanted to know why and who was responsible. That is how we became successful."

I couldn't agree more. I am a huge advocate of sales. I truly believe that the right kind of sales solves most business problems. But what you are selling needs to make sense. And by making sense I mean you need to be able to make a good profit. When businesses stray too far away from what they are good at, they often forget to consider the profitability of the projects. Can you truly remain profitable in the new market when you consider industry-specific requirements, learning curve, payment terms, etc.? Are you sure? If so, great! Go for it! But you need to know that if you are selling stuff that isn't making money, or worse yet not selling anything at all, you are destined for failure.

I could write an entire book filled with stories about operationally spectacular businesses that failed miserably. I will give you one. I met a prospect, let's call his company "Doomed LLC," that wanted us to assist him and his partners raise financing. Doomed LLC had a wonderful automotive innovation for vehicles' heating and cooling systems. This innovation would literally save this automotive OEM (original equipment manufacturer) over $5 per car. All of the partners of Doomed LLC had experience with this OEM, including numerous contacts in engineering and purchasing. Doomed LLC was in business for about two years, but unfortunately it was bleeding cash. Doomed LLC had absolutely no sales because they were waiting on an order from the OEM. The orders never came—even though they had a verifiably better product. Doomed LLC closed. The only thing the partners walked away with was massive personal credit card debt.

Although there are several lessons to be learned from the story above, I would like to focus on one. Your business needs to be profit driven. Profitpreneurship works. Here is why:

1. Entrepreneur starts/buys/inherits a business to make more money, work less hours, live by his/her rules, golf more, etc.
2. Entrepreneur invests time, money, and energy
3. Entrepreneur makes money, but is working too hard
4. Entrepreneur hires people

5. Entrepreneur and people make money
6. Entrepreneur realizes more people = more money, so entrepreneur continues to hire
7. And so on...

Obviously it is typically more complicated than this, but you get the idea. If you are still not convinced that your business needs to focus on producing cash and profits, here are some additional thoughts to consider:

1. You are likely personally guarantying some or all of the business debt
2. Your business exposes you to risk of personal economic loss
3. You often work long hours for little compensation
4. Sleepless, stress-filled nights
5. Expense accounts that you have to personally reimburse (the single thing I personally miss from working for other people)
6. You probably have successful peers that are making more money and working less hours

Profitpreneurship vs. Stupidity

Profitpreneurship does not mean gouging customers, underpaying employees, or sucking every extra dime out of your business. I would argue this is short-sighted, short-term greed. For example, I believe you need to invest in people and hire as well as you can afford. I also believe you need to invest in training and incentive-based bonuses. As the proof above illustrates, people make you money. If you do not have good people, your profits will suffer.

You may be thinking "why would a profit-driven entrepreneur hire well?" Wouldn't a profit-driven entrepreneur try to get by with the cheapest person possible? I would argue no. Obviously everyone wants to get a "deal." I am not suggesting you pay more than what should be expected for a position, but how much of a deal do you really get when you bottom-feed? The costs of training, developing, and eventually replacing a bad employee is of no benefit to the greedy entrepreneur. Sure, you can overcharge a client or fail to pay an employee commission for a short-term cash benefit. But those activities are also likely to get you fired, sued, or worse. Long-term Profitpreneurship is the way to go.

Real Investment

Profitpreneurship is critical in protecting your investment. Speaking of investment, how much have you truly invested in your business? Your true investments include both cash and debt (both business and personal debt for the benefit of the business). Let's plug in some figures for illustrative purposes:

Cash invested:	$	300,000
Debt incurred:		100,000
Total invested:	$	400,000

Based on our numbers, if your business earns $40,000 of income your Return on Investment (ROI) is equal to 10% (calculated as follows):

$40,000 / $400,000 = 10%

Not bad, even with the high rate associated with owning a small business. I think most of us would be thrilled with passive investments that showed this type of ROI (stocks, real estate, CD). However, we are not done yet. The key word of the previous statement is *passive.* Unless your business is truly passive, the above analysis is incomplete.

Opportunity Cost

Although the above illustration is a good starting point, it does not factor in the opportunity costs of the entrepreneur. Let's assume Ron (our fictional business owner from the above illustration) quit his job as a chef to buy a business. Ron no longer has the time to be fully employed outside of his business, so his income outside of work is eliminated. Aside from the sunk costs of his formal education (which he no longer utilizes), his opportunity cost is:

$50,000 base + $10,000 employee benefits = $60,000

But is Ron the only one working in the business? Not in this case. Ron's wife, Sally, helps out. She does some bookkeeping, purchasing, scheduling. She typically puts in twenty hours per week. Since the business was started, the family no longer can afford day care. Therefore, Sally quit her full-time job as an electrical engineer. Her opportunity cost is calculated as follows:

$90,000 base + $5,000 bonus + $10,000 employee benefits = $105,000 x 50% = $52,500

Using these new figures, we calculate the true ROI

Cash invested:	$	300,000
Debt incurred:		100,000
Opportunity cost:		112,500
Total invested:	$	512,500

$40,000 / $512,500 = 8%

This analysis does not even factor in the long hours, lack of vacation time, or the risk of loss associated with business ownership. Unless you are building a business that will have a market value (and eventually be sold), entrepreneurship is a huge waste of time and money.

Profit-Driven Non-Profit Organizations?

The tools and techniques described in this book are not only applicable to businesses. As non-profit and government agencies continue to become more fiscally responsible (essentially profit-driven), this book is a great playbook in making the transition. I use the terms *business* and *organization* interchangeably in this book. I ask you to do the same if you represent one of these types of organizations (replacing *business* with *organization* or *agency*). Remember non-profit is a tax status, not a goal!

Action Items
1. Calculate your real investment in your business
2. Determine how many components of the DAS Profit Process are in place at your business

CHAPTER 2: BUDGETING – SETTING POWERFUL TARGETS

"Conditions, what are conditions? I am the conditions." Napoleon Bonaparte

When Alice approaches a crossroad and asks the Cheshire Cat, sitting in the tree ahead, "Which road shall I take?" he asks, "Where do you want to go?" After Alice replies, "I don't know," he says, "Then any path will do." Alice in Wonderland

Chapter Highlights
1. Why budgeting fails
2. Creating a powerful budget
3. Using your budget to hold employees accountable
4. Using your budget to track performance

The majority of CPAs and accounting departments focus almost all of their energy on what happened. I think this emphasis on the past is flawed. Obviously it is critical to understand where you have been; however, what about the future? It is difficult to get where you want to go if your focus is on where you have been. Have you ever tried driving a car with both eyes on the rearview mirror?

Powerful Budgets

Let me ask a simple question: do you enjoy budgeting? Whether we are talking about business or personal budgeting, the answer is typically no. Most people view budgeting as a necessary evil at best. Most businesses prepare budgets simply to appease lenders or stakeholders. And if there is no such party involved, the process is simply ignored. Here are a few of the most common reasons why entrepreneurs do not like to do budgets:

1. **Budgets are wrong.** No matter how good you are at the budgeting process, it is extremely unlikely it will reflect actual results (and in most cases, the budget will be significantly different). This happens even when the creator

made a sincere effort to build an accurate budget. More often than not, owners of the business will tend to overestimate future performance in order to satisfy lenders and investors. Whereas your bean counters (accountants) will typically understate profit in order to beat the numbers.

2. **Only the owners are accountable for the numbers.** Most employees never even know what the numbers are in the budget. And when the budget is compared to actual results, it is rarely used to evaluate employees.

3. **Budgets are a waste of time.** This misconception is based on the focus of doing versus planning. Obviously I am going to try and make as much money as possible anyway, so why do I need a budget?

4. **Budgets don't serve any real management purpose.** Other than obtaining financing, the budget isn't really used for anything.

5. **Budgets are static.** They do not reflect changes that occur after the budget is complete. Whether it is a change in activity level, economic environment, or costs, the budget is not robust enough to capture these contingencies.

6. **Accountability.** Let's face it: most entrepreneurs are entrepreneurs because they do not want to be held accountable to others. Somehow committing to a budget takes away some of the entrepreneurial freedom that most business owners enjoy (or at least think they enjoy).

I am an exception. I believe a budget is one of your most powerful management tools. In addition, I truly enjoy the process. What's not to like? You are essentially building the plan to achieve your sales, profit, and cash flow goals. The trick is you need to do it the right way. When executed using the techniques described in this chapter, your budgets will become an integral tool in achieving your business goals. In addition, budgeting is actually a way to shift accountability from the business owner to others in the organization. First, let me illustrate why you should even bother doing a budget.

Stay With Me!

This part of the book may appear to be extremely technical. You may be tempted with the excuse of "this is why I have a CFO, CPA, etc." I encourage you to spend the time and try to digest as much of this chapter as possible (rereading certain parts will help). I personally feel that an entrepreneur should never rely 100 percent on their financial advisors or financial management team. If you are the one ultimately responsible for the success of your business, you need to understand the budgeting process. The goal of this chapter is to explain relatively complex concepts in a manner as simple as possible.

Nature of Costs

Let's do a quick exercise. If you have a widget manufacturing business that has $4,000,000 in sales and $400,000 net income (10% of sales), what happens if sales drop to $3,000,000? Will you still make $400,000 of income? Without drastic cost-cutting measures the answer is probably no. What about your 10%, will your business earn $300,000 of income (10% of $3,000,000)? The answer again is probably no, but for a different reason.

Fixed vs. Variable Costs

Fixed costs are expenses that generally do not change in proportion to the level of business activity. For example, my office rent is fixed for the next three years. It doesn't matter if my sales double next year, my rent payment will remain FIXED at the same amount. Variable costs by contrast change in relation to the activity of a business such as sales or production volume. If I am a retailer, variable costs include my cost of inventory costs (goods I purchase for sale). The more I sell, the more I need to buy (and the cost varies relative to the amount of sales my business generates).

So what does this mean? It means your costs of doing business can be separated into three categories: Fixed costs that almost never change over a budgetary period (e.g., rent, office salaries), variable costs that change relative to sales (e.g., material costs, sales commissions), and mixed costs that have both a fixed and variable component (e.g., utilities typically go up and down relative to production, but the portion of the utilities bill associated with the office is typically fixed because it does not change relative to the amount of production).

Now let's go back to your widget manufacturing business. Let's assume we can categorize your expenses as follows:

Sales:	$	4,000,000
Variable costs:		2,000,000
Contribution margin:		2,000,000
Fixed costs:		1,600,000
Net income:	**$**	**400,000**

Contribution margin is defined as sales minus variable costs. In our example, our variable costs are 50% of sales. This means that 50% of every dollar of sales is used to cover variable costs. The remaining 50% is used to pay for fixed costs. Whatever is left over is income (or profit). Now let's see what happens if your sales drop to $3,000,000.

Sales:	$	3,000,000
Variable costs:		1,500,000
Contribution margin:		1,500,000
Fixed costs:		1,600,000
Net loss:	**$**	**(100,000)**

The business starts losing money. The reason why is because the business does not have enough sales to cover its fixed costs. If sales dropped to zero, theoretically you will lose $1,600,000 (I say theoretically because most businesses would find a way to cut fixed costs if sales dropped that dramatically). This is one of the reasons why it is important to calculate the level at which your business breaks even (e.g., break-even analysis). Working backwards, you need to figure out the amount of sales that will produce a contribution margin equal to your fixed costs. Based on our widget manufacturer's contribution margin, we would need a minimum sales amount of $3,200,000 to break even:

Sales:	$	3,200,000
Variable costs:		1,600,000
Contribution margin:		1,600,000
Fixed costs:		1,600,000
Net income:	$	**0**

What happens after we clear the $3.2 million threshold? As one of my clients says, money drops right to the bottom line. We have a 50% contribution margin; therefore, 50% of every $1 over $3.2 million in sales drops right down to the bottom line. What happens at $5,000,000?

Sales:	$	5,000,000
Variable costs:		2,500,000
Contribution margin:		2,500,000
Fixed costs:		1,600,000
Net income:	$	**900,000**

You more than double your income if you add 25% more sales! Obviously if sales grow to a large enough amount you will eventually have to add additional fixed costs to support your growth (managers, professional fees, additional space, etc.), but this tool is intended to give you a methodology to manage your activity level. For example, this business is in a much better position to give bonuses at the $5 million mark.

Powerful Budgeting

Now that you understand some of the concepts of our budgeting process, let's take an in-depth look at our powerful budgeting process. We will start with the income statement of another widget manufacturer (Illustration IS-1).

Ren J. Carlton, CPA, CSMC

Growth, Inc.
Income Statement
April 30, 2008

	Actual	%
Revenue:	1,495,948	100.0%
Cost of Goods Sold:		
Materials	400,157	26.7%
Freight	134,265	9.0%
Labor	230,112	15.4%
Total Cost of Goods Sold	764,534	51.1%
Gross Profit	731,414	48.9%
Selling, Gen., and Admin. Expenses		
Payroll	195,642	13.1%
Bad Debts	9,500	0.6%
Travel	407	0.0%
Dues & Subscriptions	3,381	0.2%
Legal & Professional	35,540	2.4%
Utilities	18,163	1.2%
Telephone	8,262	0.6%
Rent	120,000	8.0%
Postage	5,541	0.4%
General Insurance	5,200	0.3%
Worker's Compensation Insurance	6,000	0.0%
Employee Health Insurance	34,488	2.3%
Property Tax	12,659	0.8%
State Income Tax	25,000	1.7%
Payroll Processing	2,566	0.2%
Office Supplies	7,206	0.5%
Fuel	4,048	0.3%
Depreciation	64,000	4.3%
Miscellaneous	(108)	0.0%
Total Selling, Gen., and Admin. Expenses	557,495	37.3%
Net Income	173,919	11.6%

For Management Use Only   IS-1

What does this tell you about the company? We are going to assume that the transactional accounting is being performed accurately. Gross profit seems good (49% of sales). We are profitable. Net income is almost 12% of sales, which seems pretty respectable. Many people would be happy with this performance. If you were the owner of this company, you may be tempted to pat yourself on the back and focus on the following month.

Growth, Inc.
Income Statement
April 30, 2008

	Actual	%	Budget	%	Variance	%
Revenue:	1,495,948	100.0%	1,746,000	100.0%	(250,052)	-16.7%
Cost of Goods Sold:						
Materials	400,157	26.7%	384,120	22.0%	16,037	4.0%
Freight	134,265	9.0%	104,760	6.0%	29,505	22.0%
Labor	230,112	15.4%	366,660	21.0%	(136,548)	-59.3%
Total Cost of Goods Sold	764,534	51.1%	855,540	49.0%	(91,006)	-11.9%
Gross Profit	731,414	48.9%	890,460	51.0%	(159,046)	-21.7%
Selling, Gen., and Admin. Expenses						
Payroll	195,642	13.1%	286,344	16.4%	(90,702)	-46.4%
Bad Debts	9,500	0.6%	10,000	0.6%	(500)	-5.3%
Travel	407	0.0%	3,400	0.2%	(2,993)	-735.2%
Dues & Subscriptions	3,381	0.2%	1,000	0.1%	2,381	70.4%
Legal & Professional	35,540	2.4%	10,600	0.6%	24,940	70.2%
Utilities	18,163	1.2%	17,460	1.0%	703	3.9%
Telephone	8,262	0.6%	6,600	0.4%	1,662	20.1%
Rent	120,000	8.0%	120,000	6.9%	-	0.0%
Postage	5,541	0.4%	5,100	0.3%	441	8.0%
General Insurance	5,200	0.3%	6,400	0.4%	(1,200)	-23.1%
Worker's Compensation Insurance	6,000	0.0%	3,200	0.2%	2,800	46.7%
Employee Health Insurance	34,488	2.3%	31,500	1.8%	2,988	8.7%
Property Tax	12,659	0.8%	16,500	0.9%	(3,841)	-30.3%
State Income Tax	25,000	1.7%	4,200	0.2%	20,800	83.2%
Payroll Processing	2,566	0.2%	2,300	0.1%	266	10.4%
Office Supplies	7,206	0.5%	12,000	0.7%	(4,794)	-66.5%
Fuel	4,048	0.3%	3,492	0.2%	556	13.7%
Depreciation	64,000	4.3%	64,000	3.7%	-	0.0%
Miscellaneous	(108)	0.0%	900	0.1%	(1,008)	932.4%
Total Selling, Gen., and Admin. Expenses	557,495	37.3%	604,996	34.7%	(47,501)	-8.5%
Net Income	173,919	11.6%	285,464	16.3%	(111,545)	-64.1%

For Management Use Only   IS-2

Illustration IS-2 takes us a little bit deeper. We are comparing this month's performance to the annual budget. We have taken the annual budget for the company and divided all of the figures by 12 (in order to calculate monthly budgeted numbers). This methodology assumes even sales and costs throughout the year. Based on this budget, it appears that sales are less than expected. It also appears that net income is significantly less than expected (64 percent less than expected). What initially appeared to be a good month now looks mediocre at best. Where is our controller? I want an explanation!

Growth, Inc.
Income Statement
April 30, 2008

	Actual	%	Budget	%	Variance	%
Revenue:						
Actual	1,495,948		1,746,000		(250,052)	-16.7%
Adjusted for ABC comparison	1,495,948	100.0%	1,495,948	100.0%		
Cost of Goods Sold/Variable Costs:						
Materials	400,157	26.7%	329,109	22.0%	71,048	17.8%
Freight	134,265	9.0%	89,757	6.0%	44,508	33.1%
Labor	230,112	15.4%	314,149	21.0%	(84,037)	-36.5%
Total Cost of Goods Sold/Variable Costs	764,534	51.1%	733,015	49.0%	31,519	4.1%
Gross Profit/Contribution Margin	731,414	48.9%	762,933	51.0%	(31,519)	-4.3%
S, G, and A Expenses/Fixed Costs						
Payroll	195,642	13.1%	286,344	19.1%	(90,702)	-46.4%
Bad Debts	9,500	0.6%	10,000	0.7%	(500)	-5.3%
Travel	407	0.0%	3,400	0.2%	(2,993)	-735.2%
Dues & Subscriptions	3,381	0.2%	1,000	0.1%	2,381	70.4%
Legal & Professional	35,540	2.4%	10,600	0.7%	24,940	70.2%
Utilities	18,163	1.2%	17,460	1.2%	703	3.9%
Telephone	8,262	0.6%	6,600	0.4%	1,662	20.1%
Rent	120,000	8.0%	120,000	8.0%	-	0.0%
Postage	5,541	0.4%	5,100	0.3%	441	8.0%
General Insurance	5,200	0.3%	6,400	0.4%	(1,200)	-23.1%
Worker's Compensation Insurance	6,000	0.0%	3,200	0.2%	2,800	46.7%
Employee Health Insurance	34,488	2.3%	31,500	2.1%	2,988	8.7%
Property Tax	12,659	0.8%	16,500	1.1%	(3,841)	-30.3%
State Income Tax	25,000	1.7%	4,200	0.3%	20,800	83.2%
Payroll Processing	2,566	0.2%	2,300	0.2%	266	10.4%
Office Supplies	7,206	0.5%	12,000	0.8%	(4,794)	-66.5%
Fuel	4,048	0.3%	3,492	0.2%	556	13.7%
Depreciation	64,000	4.3%	64,000	4.3%	-	0.0%
Miscellaneous	(108)	0.0%	900	0.1%	(1,008)	932.4%
Total S, G, and A Expenses/Fixed Costs	557,495	37.3%	604,996	40.4%	(47,501)	-8.5%
Net Income	173,919	11.6%	157,937	10.6%	15,982	9.2%

For Management Use Only   IS-3

In Illustration IS-3, we are comparing our actual results to an activity-based budget. This methodology accounts for the differences in variable and fixed costs. When sales decline, so should the corresponding variable costs—while fixed costs remain the same. In our illustration, we are assuming that the expenses in our costs of goods sold are variable. We also are assuming that our selling, general, and administrative (S, G, and A) costs are fixed.

Although it is blatantly obvious that sales are a concern in our example, it is not the only aspect of the business needing attention. Activity-based budgeting gives you a tool to objectively analyze those other areas of your business. As you can see in our analysis, gross profit is down by 4.3 percent relative to where it should be at that sales level. If you look at the previous illustration (IS-2), an operations manager may simply say "of course gross profit is down, look at sales!" If you use Illustration IS-3, that excuse no longer works. Sales are obviously a primary concern, but operations need to step up as well!

Growth, Inc.
Income Statement
April 30, 2008

	Variance	%		Notes
Revenue:				
Actual	(250,052)	-16.7%	AE	Reduced orders because of Axel Motors strike
Adjusted for ABC comparison				
Cost of Goods Sold/Variable Costs:				
Materials	71,048	17.8%	JS	Increase due to retroactive price increase
Freight	44,508	33.1%	JS	Increase in fuel charges
Labor	(84,037)	-36.5%	JS	Layoffs
Total Cost of Goods Sold/Variable Costs	31,519	4.1%		
Gross Profit/Contribution Margin	(31,519)	-4.3%		
S, G, and A Expenses/Fixed Costs				
Payroll	(90,702)	-46.4%	JS	Layoffs
Bad Debts	(500)	-5.3%	AE	
Travel	(2,993)	-735.2%	AE	
Dues & Subscriptions	2,381	70.4%	DC	
Legal & Professional	24,940	70.2%	RS	Additional legal fees from ATS lawsuit
Utilities	703	3.9%	JS	
Telephone	1,662	20.1%	DC	
Rent	-	0.0%	DC	
Postage	441	8.0%	DC	
General Insurance	(1,200)	-23.1%	DC	
Worker's Compensation Insurance	2,800	46.7%	MK	
Employee Health Insurance	2,988	8.7%	MK	
Property Tax	(3,841)	-30.3%	DC	
State Income Tax	20,800	83.2%	DC	Prior year tax payment made with extension
Payroll Processing	266	10.4%	DC	
Office Supplies	(4,794)	-66.5%	DC	
Fuel	556	13.7%	JS	
Depreciation	-	0.0%	DC	
Miscellaneous	(1,008)	932.4%	DC	
Total S, G, and A Expenses/Fixed Costs	(47,501)	-8.5%		
Net Income	15,982	9.2%		

Variance Threshold: Under/over $15,000 and 10%.

For Management Use Only IS-4

Illustration IS-4 is an activity-based budget on steroids! Not only are you getting your actual results compared to a robust activity-based budget, you are also getting an explanation of significant variances. This comparison also identifies the individuals responsible for each of the line items on your income statement (by listing their initials). If you have a question, you (or better yet your profit team) know who to talk to. Assuming you communicated the budget to these individuals, they should be ready with a good explanation.

Building Your Powerful Budget

Now let's discuss the steps in building your powerful budget.

> Step 1 – Setting the Targets
> Step 2 – Build Initial 12-Month Budget
> Step 3 – Create Activity-Based Budget
> Step 4 – Build Three Budgets

Step 5 – Line-Item Accountability
Step 6 – Set Explanation Threshold
Step 7 – Monthly Budgetary Meeting

Step 1 – Setting the Targets – Why "The Secret" does not work

This is tricky. Let's start with a quick story. I, along with millions of others, have read the book *The Secret.* From my understanding, the message is to write stuff down. If you write it down, it will happen (again, my interpretation of the message). After I read this, I could not believe the power I unleashed. All my problems were solved! I decided to try my newfound abilities at golf. I was ready. I was pumped. I was positive. I wrote it down.

"I will shoot a 72 today."

My handicap is around an 18. In case you are not familiar with golf, a 72 is a really good score. An 18 handicap barely qualifies me to hold up the "Quiet Please" sign while professional golfers take their swings on TV.

It didn't matter. I now knew "The Secret." I was pumped. I was positive. I wrote it down.

I positively shot a 98.

Not bad, but not good. I typically shoot around a 95. It sure wasn't a 72. What gives? What happened to "The Secret"? You mean I am not going to be able to shoot a 72 by just writing it down?

Don't get me wrong, I actually think *The Secret* has a lot to offer. But I also believe it misrepresents the simplicity of goal achievement. Writing it down is critical. But no matter how many times I write down "I will shoot a 72 today," it is extremely unlikely to happen on a regulation eighteen-hole golf course. Is it because of my weak mind? Lack of resolve? Lack of faith?

No, it is the fact that the goal is not rooted in reality. I am a much better golfer when I play as a bogey golfer. This means I assume it will take me one more stroke than what is considered par. So if it is a par 4, I will assume it will take me five strokes to get the ball to the hole. This changes my entire strategy. I take less risky shots, because now I have a cushion. Don't get me wrong, I still dream of shooting par golf (and occasionally I have holes where I do make a par or better). However, I play for bogey. If I were consistently a bogey golfer, my handicap would improve. Bogey golf is currently my stretch goal (we will discuss stretch goals in depth a little bit later).

Applying this message to your budgeting process, your budget targets need to be:

1. Realistic
2. Optimistic
3. Inspirational

Realistic

I am a huge believer in stretch goals, but not unrealistic goals. You can "budget" for anything you want, but it needs be close to realistic expectations. If you think you should do $10 million in sales next year, target $11 million. If you are on track for $50,000 in income, budget $70,000.

Optimistic

You need to be optimistic, but optimistic within the constraints of reality. You probably should not assume you will get every large contract you pursue, but isn't it likely you will get some of them? What about new efforts? How will efficiencies improve now that your staff has been with you another year? What initiatives will you launch? All of these variables need to be factored into your budget.

Inspirational

Inspirational is critical. Does the target excite you? Will it encourage you to work late and get up early? Will it motivate your staff? Complacency is the kiss of death to any business. Inspirational goals are a great way to challenge and engage your best and brightest. I just don't get when companies budget for losses or flat/declining sales. It must be tough inspiring your team with the war cry of "let's go out there and lose half as much money as we did last month!" The true power of "The Secret" is to inspire, but within reason. Otherwise, what's the point?

Step 2 – Build Initial 12-Month Budget

I typically start off by projecting sales. I believe revenue drives all decisions. Follow the revenue, and everything else will follow. Talk to your marketing manager and salespeople (or to yourself if you are the only salesperson). What is in the pipeline? What is on the horizon? Don't forget you are talking to salespeople. Make sure they are committed, because ultimately they are the ones that will (or should) be accountable. I realize budgeting sales can be tough, like the old saying says:

I know that half of my advertising dollars are wasted … I just don't know which half." John Wanamaker

We use historical data. As any wealth advisor will tell you, the past does not guaranty future performance. That being said, it is typically a good starting point, especially if you have a reoccurring revenue model. Then I make assumptions based on the addition/removal of marketing activities, as well as changes in the industry and economic environment. If our client uses outside marketing vendors (agencies, consultants, etc.), we ask them what return they should expect from the investment. And most importantly, we build measurement tools and metrics to track their performance.

Don't get too hung up on industry or economic statistics. Unless you have 100 percent market penetration, a 5 percent reduction in your industry does not necessarily impact your business. I have a client whose CFO's budget is entirely based on the industry's projected activity for the year. If the industry is "projected" to have a 4 percent drop in revenue, then the CFO projects the same for my client's business (until we convince him otherwise). This particular client has about 3 percent of the market. What about proactive marketing? Stealing clients from the competition? Cross-selling opportunities? The opportunities are endless.

Another sales projection technique I feel the need to rebuke is the fallacy of large numbers. It goes something like this. If I open a pizza parlor in the city of Troy, which has approximately 70,000 people, I cannot fail. I will likely get at least one out of five residents to come to my parlor twice per year. That equates to 28,000 orders. Our average order is $20, so we should have at least $560,000 in first year sales! I have seen this logic applied to numerous business scenarios (especially Internet-based businesses where you have millions of so-called prospects). It is simply flawed logic. In the above scenario, it is also possible that you will only get one out of 5,000 residents to place a single order. You simply cannot project without more marketing data.

Once you have projected sales for twelve months, the next step is gross profit (Sales – Cost of Goods Sold). Gross profit (as a percentage of sales) typically remains relatively consistent UNLESS you have some form of operational initiatives in mind (e.g., waste reduction, training, technological advances). Don't forget about inflation and raises. Talk to your operations people and managers, and make sure they understand that they will be accountable for their accuracy.

Finally, take care of your selling, general, and administrative expenses. Again, start off by looking at last year. Another method is a zero-based budgeting approach. This technique advocates starting with a clean slate every year. Personally I think that adds unnecessary work. We simply use last year's information and make the applicable adjustments for cost increases/decreases (e.g., staff additions/reductions, new marketing campaigns).

Ren J. Carlton, CPA, CSMC

Step 3 – Create Activity-Based Budget Template

Here is where you build in the flexibility. In order to do so, you need to identify which of your costs are fixed, which are variable, and which are mixed. Once you are able to do so, then you need to assign a sales factor to each variable cost (e.g., materials are 20 percent of sales). Although you should take your time constructing this financial model, it will never be perfect. If you are not sure a line item should be 1 percent or 1.5 percent, pick one and be done with it. Remember, budgeting is always an estimate. The important thing is that you use reasonable assumptions.

Mixed costs can be handled multiple ways. You can split the variable and fixed components into two separate line items on your income statement (e.g., one line for the variable component of utilities and one line for the fixed component of utilities). Or you can simply designate a cost as variable or fixed, based on which category would be the most accurate. Again, it will never be perfect.

In my illustrations, I assumed that all of the cost-of-goods-sold expenses were variable and all my selling, general, and administrative expenses were fixed. Doing this simplifies the process, because gross profit equals contribution margin. If this is not a reasonable methodology for your business, I recommend preparing a separate management report that looks something like Illustration IS-5.

Growth, Inc.
Income Statement
April 30, 2008

	Actual	%	Budget	%	Variance	%	
Revenue:							
Actual	1,495,948		1,746,000		(250,052)	-16.7%	AE
Adjusted for ABC comparison	1,495,948	100.0%	1,495,948	100.0%			
Variable Costs:							
Materials	400,157	26.7%	329,109	22.0%	71,048	17.8%	JS
Freight	134,265	9.0%	89,757	6.0%	44,508	33.1%	JS
Labor	230,112	15.4%	314,149	21.0%	(84,037)	-36.5%	JS
Payroll	195,642	13.1%	245,335	16.4%	(49,693)	-25.4%	JS
Utilities	18,163	1.2%	14,959	1.0%	3,204	17.6%	JS
Fuel	4,048	0.3%	2,992	0.2%	1,056	26.1%	JS
Total Variable Costs	982,387	65.7%	996,301	66.6%	(13,914)	-1.4%	
Contribution Margin	513,561	34.3%	499,647	33.4%	13,914	2.7%	
Fixed Costs							
Bad Debts	9,500	0.6%	10,000	0.7%	(500)	-5.3%	AE
Travel	407	0.0%	3,400	0.2%	(2,993)	-735.2%	AE
Dues & Subscriptions	3,381	0.2%	1,000	0.1%	2,381	70.4%	DC
Legal & Professional	35,540	2.4%	10,600	0.7%	24,940	70.2%	RS
Telephone	8,262	0.6%	6,600	0.4%	1,662	20.1%	DC
Rent	120,000	8.0%	120,000	8.0%	-	0.0%	DC
Postage	5,541	0.4%	5,100	0.3%	441	8.0%	DC
General Insurance	5,200	0.3%	6,400	0.4%	(1,200)	-23.1%	DC
Worker's Compensation Insurance	6,000	0.0%	3,200	0.2%	2,800	46.7%	MK
Employee Health Insurance	34,488	2.3%	31,500	2.1%	2,988	8.7%	MK
Property Tax	12,659	0.8%	16,500	1.1%	(3,841)	-30.3%	DC
State Income Tax	25,000	1.7%	4,200	0.3%	20,800	83.2%	DC
Payroll Processing	2,566	0.2%	2,300	0.2%	266	10.4%	DC
Office Supplies	7,206	0.5%	12,000	0.8%	(4,794)	-66.5%	DC
Depreciation	64,000	4.3%	64,000	4.3%	-	0.0%	DC
Miscellaneous	(108)	0.0%	900	0.1%	(1,008)	932.4%	DC
Total Fixed Costs	339,642	22.7%	297,700	19.9%	41,942	12.3%	
Net Income	173,919	11.6%	201,947	13.5%	(28,028)	-16.1%	

Variance Threshold: Under/over $15,000 and 10%.

For Management Use Only   IS-5

As you can see, some of our selling, general, and administrative expenses are now in the variable cost section. Determining if your business requires this level of analysis is based purely on preference. If this widget company was my client, I think this schedule would be excessive. I would argue Illustration IS-4 gives sufficient information. But again, it is your business. You need to make the decision.

Step 4 – Build Three Budgets

Now that you have created your budgeting template, I recommend building three monthly budgets—which should be simple since you already built your monthly budgeting template. The first is the "Break-Even" budget. This budget simply illustrates the amount of sales necessary to achieve $0 income. When you are done, the format should be similar to the budget column in Illustration IS-3 with net income as close to zero as possible.

The second budget is the "Likely" budget. This is where you really think you are going to end up on a monthly basis. It should be optimistic, but also extremely realistic.

The third is your "Stretch" budget. This should illustrate what happens if almost everything goes right. It should still be realistic, but extremely optimistic. This is the inspirational budget you will use to fire up your staff.

I frequently am asked which budget I should use for which purpose. Generally speaking, I use the Stretch budget for setting staff goals, the Likely budget for the bank, and the Break-Even as an internal sanity check. However, there are exceptions. I have a client that went through a tough year. In order to attract a new lender (which we were being forced to do by their current bank), we needed to put some "lipstick on that pig" before we took it to market. Part of the lipstick was the Stretch budget.

You can also use your template to run a wide variety of what-if analyses, including capital expenditures evaluation, ROI for an acquisition/divestiture, impact of hiring/firing employees, etc.

Step 5 – Line-Item Accountability

This is one of the most important steps in your budgeting process, even though it is often skipped. One of the reasons that most budgeting processes fall short is because of the lack of accountability.

One of our clients' CFO once commented that it was unfair for him to be held accountable for the financial performance of the company. Although he was supposedly responsible for expenditures, several shareholders and managers had the ability to approve expenses in their departments. When it came time to report on the numbers, expenses were always way out of line. Since the CFO had no power to restrict these expenses, he felt helpless.

Line-item accountability can eliminate this problem. You designate a person responsible for each line item of your budget (as shown in Illustrations IS-4 and IS-5). Not only is this person accountable, this person must have the ability to approve or reject these types of expenses. For example, you cannot designate your CFO in charge of accounting fees unless he or she is responsible for hiring and managing the services from the outside accounting firm. Failure to delegate the authority over these expenses would be both ineffective and unfair. You should also consider the opinion of the responsible person when setting the budgeted dollar amount. It is much easier to ensure accountability if the accountable person is involved in the budgetary process.

Personally I believe it is important for the CEO to have as few line-items as possible (if any). I understand that this may seem like an unrealistic task for smaller businesses; however, I would challenge every CEO to at least try. The CEO's role is to hire and manage a team to run the organization. It is also the CEO's role to help the management team hit their goals (when assistance is required). It is not the CEO's role to serve as chief, cook, and bottle-washer. It is difficult, if not impossible, to run a business when the bulk of your time is spent in the details. And if your management team is incapable of handling their management roles, it is time to hire a new team.

This accountability should trickle down through the entire organization. If your sales manager is responsible for producing $5,000,000 in revenue over a certain period, each of his direct reports should be responsible for a portion of that $5,000,000. And if the goal is not achieved, it is the sales manager's job to deal with the applicable salespeople accordingly. But it is the sales manager's fault for having non-performing salespeople on his team. And it is ultimately the CEO's fault because she has a non-performing sales manager on her team! Again, it is important to emphasize the necessity for delegating authority. It is only fair that the sales manager has hire, fire, train, and reward authority over his team. Otherwise it is difficult to hold the sales manager accountable for the performance of the sales team.

Step 6 – Set Explanation Threshold

As shown in Illustrations IS-4 and IS-5, some line items on our Budget-to-Actual Comparison have notes. These notes explain the significant variances between actual results and our budgeted amounts. These notes also force the accountable individuals to acknowledge the discrepancy, as well as explain what is going on to the CEO.

The amount of variance considered significant is determined on a company-by-company basis. In our example, our variance threshold is "Under/over $15,000 and 10%." This means we require an explanation from the person responsible for a line item that is both:

1. 10% over or under budget
2. Over or under budget by $15,000

In our illustration, we use both under/over $15,000 and 10%, but you may prefer to use either. It is simply a matter of what is important enough to you to require an explanation. Using our example, you may not be comfortable with a phone bill that is 20% over budget—even though the amount of the variance is only 0.1% of monthly sales.

Setting the thresholds can be tricky. The dollar amount and percentage you choose for your business is entirely up to you. At our firm and in our example, we use approximately 1% of monthly sales for the dollar threshold and 10% for the percentage threshold. This methodology makes it easy to apply our process to both smaller and larger businesses. For example, a business with $100,000 in monthly sales would research items that were over or under budget by $1,000 (and over/under by 10%).

You may be tempted to require explanations on almost every variance (e.g., variances over/under 2 percent). I would argue that it is important to focus on the significant deviations from your budget. If everything is a priority, nothing is. For example, do you really care if office supplies are 4 percent over budget if sales are down 20 percent? If something is bugging you outside the threshold, you can always follow up with the responsible person; however, your focus should be on the large outliers, at least initially.

It is important to mention that you need to obtain explanation for both favorable and unfavorable variances. You may be thinking (per Illustration IS-4), "Why should I investigate payroll being $90,000 under budget? Isn't that a good thing?" The answer is possibly. It is also possible that it is an indicator of a problem (e.g., missing invoice, employees sandbagging when setting the budget). It is important to question found money.

To illustrate the above point, we had a client with a very happy controller ("Fred"). He received a tax refund check from the IRS for approximately $80,000. He proudly walked into the owner's office and placed the check on the owner's desk. After calling me into the office, the conversation went something like this:

Owner: "That's great! We could use $80,000."
Ren: "Why did you get a refund from the IRS? It isn't in our budget."
Fred: "I'm not sure."
Ren: "Don't you think it's important to know?"
Fred: "I don't really understand the correspondence, but does it matter?"
Ren: "Yes!"
Fred: "We don't want any trouble from the IRS, so we typically pay any bills they send. I figure we must have overpaid something at one point. Just so you know, Ren, we have never been audited."

Ren: "That's great, but let's investigate to make sure. Whatever you do, don't cash the check."
Fred: "Are you nuts! We need this cash."
Ren: "Give my company a couple days. I will have a definitive answer for you then."

Upon further investigation, we determined that our client had made an error with their payroll tax payments. This client had multiple entities. Their controller made some of their payroll tax payments using the wrong Tax Identification Number. This caused our client to grossly overpay the payroll taxes for one of their entities (by approximately $80,000) and grossly underpay the payroll taxes of another entity (by approximately $80,000). After several letters and conversations with IRS agents, we were able to resolve this issue and avoid the massive interest and penalties that would have resulted in cashing that check.

Step 7 – Monthly Budgetary Meeting

Now that you have your budgetary process built, it needs to be followed on a monthly basis. Ideally you hold a monthly budgetary meeting within fifteen days of month-end. At this meeting you need to review the previous month's results, obtain an understanding of the significant budget-to-actual variances, congratulate or reprimand the applicable individuals (based on their performance), and discuss changes that need to be made. If you did all of the above steps properly, the data should speak for itself.

Commitment

Miyagi: "Now, ready?"
Daniel: "I guess so."
Miyagi: "Man walk on road. Walk left side, safe. Walk right side, safe. Walk down middle, sooner or later, get squished* [makes squish gesture] *just like grape. Same here; you karate do 'yes' or karate do 'no.' You karate do 'guess so,'* [makes squish gesture] *just like grape. Understand?"*
Daniel LaRusso (Ralph Macchio) and Mr. Miyagi (Pat Morita), *The Karate Kid*

The reason I call our budgeting process powerful is because it is. Our budgeting process will impact your entire organization if executed properly. It will highlight the good, the bad, and the ugly. In case you are unaware, the wrong type of people DO NOT WANT TO BE ACCOUNTABLE! They will fight. They will tell you it is a waste of time, money, energy, resources, etc. They will say they are too busy. Ultimately the CEO has to make the decision. Do you want a profit-driven organization? If so, prepare for the push back. Everyone thinks they want to be on a winning team. But do you have what it takes to lead your team to victory?

Our firm is extremely successful in implementing the techniques in this book. The times we are unsuccessful are almost always attributable to a weak CEO. When I say weak I mean weak in his or her conviction to implement our methodologies. We had one client where the CEO's two partners had a different excuse every week for not wanting us involved in their business. It was a bad time of year, their industry was in trouble, they could do it themselves, our fees were too high, they needed more time, they couldn't fire people because they would get sued, etc. Ultimately we were terminated and the engagement failed (as well as the business a year later!).

One of my favorite types of engagements is when the CEO hires us to be the "bad guy." The CEO has an idea of what needs to be done, but is not in the position to implement the changes (does not feel comfortable being the bad guy, sensitivity due to a recent merger, family members working in the business, fellow stakeholders, etc.). I love this role because we are enabled to be as blunt and direct as necessary. The funny thing is this method almost always saves our client money. We spend less time on politics, which results in achieving faster results.

If you decide you want a profit-driven business, it is important to commit, whether on your own with or with my firm's help. Otherwise get squished just like grape!

Now that you have your budgets in place, it is time to execute!

Action Items

1. Create your activity-based budget template
2. Build three budgets for your business (Break-Even, Likely, and Stretch)
3. Assign employees to each line item of your budget
4. Monitor budget-to-actual performance on a monthly basis

CHAPTER 3: DASHBOARDS – THE NUMBERS THAT DRIVE YOUR BUSINESS

"If you feel everything is under control, you are not going fast enough!" Mario Andretti

Chapter Highlights
1. Monitoring your company's vital signs
2. Building a dashboard for your business
3. Common metrics for monitoring performance

Now that you have your budget in place, how do you make sure you achieve your targeted results? Although our budgeting process is powerful, it is not enough. It is important to know what happened last month, but what happened last week? It is now time to build your weekly dashboard:

Dashboards

Before we started building dashboards, clients would frequently ask us a number of questions on a regular basis. How much cash do we have? How much can I spend? How are sales this year? How are we doing relative to last year? How are we doing relative to our budget? What do I owe the bank? What is my business worth?

As an entrepreneur, I could relate. These are the numbers that kept me up at night. We decided providing this information on an ad hoc basis was not effective. So we implemented the use of weekly dashboards. And our clients loved them!

The goal of the weekly dashboard is to report the critical metrics regarding the business on a regular basis, typically weekly. Although preparing weekly dashboards can be a time-consuming exercise, knowing the key metrics about your business is critical. And not what those metrics were four weeks ago, but rather what those numbers are today! We often refer to our dashboard as a Tahiti Report. If the business owner was on vacation in Tahiti, what information would he or she want to know in order to understand exactly what was going on with his or her business?

Below are the typical metrics we utilize. Your business may do it differently, but Illustration D-1 is one of our typical dashboards.

		Actual	Budget	Prior Year
Cash	In bank	$ 1,000,000	$ 850,000	$ 600,000
	Available for use	760,000	646,000	456,000
	Available for discretionary expenses	577,600	490,960	346,560
Sales	Year-to-date	$ 15,000,000	$ 12,500,000	$ 10,000,000
	Month-to-date	12,300,000	10,250,000	8,200,000
Profit	**Gross Profit**			
	Year-to-date	$ 9,000,000	$ 7,500,000	$ 6,000,000
	Month-to-date	7,380,000	6,150,000	4,920,000
	Net Income			
	Year-to-date	$ 3,750,000	$ 3,125,000	$ 2,500,000
	Month-to-date	3,075,000	2,562,500	2,050,000
	EBITDA			
	Year-to-date	$ 4,500,000	$ 3,750,000	$ 3,000,000
	Month-to-date	3,690,000	3,075,000	2,460,000
Accounts Receivable	Total	$ 1,875,000	$ 1,562,500	$ 1,250,000
	Under 30 days	656,250	546,875	437,500
	Over 90 days	93,750	78,125	62,500
	Reserve for doubtful accounts	56,250	46,875	37,500
Accounts Payable	Total	$ 1,687,500	$ 1,406,250	$ 1,125,000
	Under 30 days	590,625	492,188	393,750
	Over 90 days	-	-	56,250
Debt	Total bank debt	$ 4,500,000	$ 3,750,000	$ 3,000,000
	Total non-bank third party debt	900,000	750,000	600,000
	Debt due in 30 days	75,000	62,500	50,000
	Debt due < year	900,000	750,000	600,000
	Debt due > year	3,600,000	3,000,000	2,400,000
Equity	Net book value	$ 6,750,000	$ 5,625,000	$ 4,500,000
	Estimated valuation	18,000,000	15,000,000	12,000,000
	Estimated net fair market value	12,600,000	10,500,000	8,400,000

Growth Inc.
Weekly Dashboard
April 2010

For Management Use Only   D-1

For the majority of the metrics we monitor, we want to know what the number was at the end of the previous week, what we budgeted the number to be, and what the number was last year at the same time. This gives the entrepreneur the ability to know where the business is today, where it was last year, and how the business is doing relative to the business plan. The key to building a good dashboard is simplicity. The information needs to be current, accurate, and relevant to the business owner. Here are the numbers I consider critical to almost any business.

Cash

Cash is your most important resource. We categorize cash in terms of what is in the bank (per your bank statements), what is available for use (book balance), and what we have for discretionary expenses. Our dashboards report this information.

Sales

Sales are the primary driver for long-term decision making. We typically track both year-to-date and month-to-date sales. You can also track sales by division, product line, etc. It depends on what is meaningful to you.

Profit

Profit is the measurement of business success (or failure!). Income measures overall profitability, gross profit reports operational performance, and EBITDA (Earnings Before Interest, Taxes, Depreciation, and Amortization) measures cash flow. These measurements are also used by lenders and investors when valuing a business. Similar to sales, I like to see both year-to-date and month-to-date profit information.

Accounts Receivable

Monitoring your accounts receivable ensures your collections are under control. I like entrepreneurs to know what their clients owe them and what portion of their receivables are current (under thirty days). It is also important to understand what receivables are in danger of not being collected (over ninety days). If you have bank debt with covenants, receivables that are over ninety days old are typically ineligible for borrowing because of their risk of default.

Understanding which receivables are likely to be written off is also important.

Accounts Payable

Knowing how much money you owe your vendors is also important. Similar to monitoring your Accounts Receivable, you should know the total, what is current (under thirty days), and what is grossly delinquent (over ninety days). Realize that your payables over ninety days are ineligible for credit from your vendors' banks. This can cause credit hold, ruining of your company's credit rating, and possibly a collections lawsuit.

Debt

How much money do you owe your lenders? How much do you owe this month? This year? On our dashboards, we differentiate between the bank and non-bank debt (due to the difference in lending requirements). In most circumstances, bank debt tends to be much more stringent than non-bank debt (e.g., debt from friends, family, and/or stakeholders). Non-bank debt may not require payments, interest, etc. Bank debt typically has much stricter payment terms and restrictions.

Equity

Equity is a measure of what your business is worth. There are numerous ways to value a business. The most applicable methodology depends on the size and type of business you are in. Net book value is simply the difference between the assets and liabilities of your company. If you own more than you owe, it is positive (which is good). If you owe more than you own, your net book value is negative (which is bad). For most companies, net book value is not a true value of the company. More applicable methodologies include income approaches (multiple of earnings or cash flow), asset-based approaches (fair market value of the company assets), and market approaches (comparable business sales). Consult your CPA for the applicable methodology for estimating your company's true value.

Making Your Dashboard

The example above is simply a sample of what our standard dashboard looks like. Feel free to customize it for your business. For example, resellers and manufacturers probably want to monitor inventory (e.g., inventory cost, inventory value, purchases/sales in the next thirty days). If you do not have debt, obviously you do not need to measure this metric. Some owners want to see ratios. Other entrepreneurs like to monitor growth/decline over the prior month, quarter, or year. The important thing is to report what is important and meaningful to you on a weekly basis.

It is also important to note that getting your critical numbers is not always simple. Don't restrict yourself to the easily accessible information. Measuring what is important is what counts. Have you ever driven a car without a fuel gauge? I did when I was in college. My "beater" car generally got me from point A to point B, but I ran out of gas numerous times (which my wife can attest to). I would argue that fuel level is one of the critical numbers for effectively operating a vehicle. What are the critical numbers you need to effectively operate your business?

Action Items
1. Identify the numbers that drive your business
2. Build your company's dashboard
3. Develop a process to produce your company dashboard on a weekly basis

CHAPTER 4: EMPLOYEE SCORECARDS – MAXIMIZING EMPLOYEE PERFORMANCE

"Opportunity is missed by most people because it is dressed in overalls and looks like work." Thomas A. Edison

"What gets measured gets managed." Peter Drucker

Chapter Highlights
1. Creating employee accountability
2. Identifying the employee activities that truly create value for your business
3. Implementing an employee scorecard system
4. Sample scorecard information for various areas of business

No one is ever going to care like the owners. But can you steer activity to make your employees act like owners? Turn the lights off, stop idling trucks in the winter, ask if you can afford that raise/ bonus? Everyone thinks they want to be on a winning team, but not everyone is willing to do what it takes to win. How can you identify the true winners on your team?

What's Your Number?

Every employee should have a scorecard. A scorecard reports two to five metrics for each individual in your organization. These numbers are used to evaluate performance. The scorecard should illustrate the goal for each metric, as well as the individual's performance (or number) for each metric.

Employee scorecard frequency can vary. You can do weekly, monthly, quarterly, and/or annually. It depends on the importance of the metric in question. It may also make sense to do multiple scorecards (e.g., using weekly scorecards for the most timely metrics, monthly for the lesser timely metrics.) For example, billable hours are critical to professional services companies. They impact scheduling, deadlines, hiring/firing, and cost. Most professional service businesses cannot effectively run their businesses looking at billable hour data once per month. They need it weekly. The rest of their employee metrics can be properly managed on a monthly basis.

Each business is different. The key is to identify the activities you want to encourage, determine an acceptable level of performance for each of these activities, and then create a numerical methodology to report this information on a regular basis. Illustration S-1 shows a simple version of a divisional scorecard.

Growth Inc.
Production Scorecards
April, 2010

Johnson

	Monthly Goal	April, 2010	Variance
Widgets Produced	90,000	92,250	2,250
Rejects/Defects	450	461	(11)
Overtime Hours	-	-	-

Smith

	Monthly Goal	April, 2010	Variance
Widgets Produced	90,000	88,922	(1,078)
Rejects/Defects	450	445	5
Overtime Hours	-	24	24

Williams

	Monthly Goal	April, 2010	Variance
Widgets Produced	90,000	100,010	10,010
Rejects/Defects	450	300	150
Overtime Hours	-	-	-

For Management Use Only   S-1

Scorecard Presentation

As far as presentation of the results, I prefer the use of one report to illustrate all of the scorecards for each level of your organization (e.g., staff-level employee scorecards, another report to display manager-level scorecards). Even if some of the individual metrics vary, I like this methodology because it creates peer pressure.

It shows everyone how everyone else on the team is performing. It also shows how much each individual employee is contributing to the overall performance of the business. This open-book policy is purely a preference. You can also choose to report scorecards individually, by department, by geographic region, etc.

Some clients feel it is inappropriate to communicate managers' performances to their subordinates. I tend to agree. It sends the message that everyone is treated equally. This is simply not the case. Managers have greater perks, but they also have greater responsibilities. A manager's performance is the responsibility of his or her superiors, not his or her subordinates. Again, you can do what you want with your scorecards. But I think it makes more sense if managers are all on one scorecard, executives are on another, etc.

Scorecard Implementation

This is our process for implementing scorecards for our clients.
1. Identify Metrics
2. Set Targets
3. Communicate Results
4. Manage Employees to Metrics

Step 1: Identify Metrics

In selecting the numbers, you need to make sure they are
1. Applicable Activities
2. Quantifiable
3. Controllable

Applicable Activities

You should aim to monitor the activities you want to encourage. How do you pick these applicable activities? Again, these should be the activities you want to encourage, not necessarily the easiest activities to measure. Just like your dashboard, measuring what is important is not always simple. What are the primary activities for your individual employees that drive success—both for them and your business? Those are the activities that must be monitored and managed.

Not all metrics are created equal. If that is the case for your business, I suggest you weigh your metrics. For example, you may rate a salesperson 70 percent on sales and 30 percent on the profitability of those sales. In our previous example, we identified billable hours as a critical metric for professional service businesses. Even though it is one of their most important management metrics, should it be the most heavily weighted?

Billable hours is typically how most employees are measured at professional services businesses. Since it is tied to customer billing, billable hour information is almost always readily accessible. The problem is that it isn't always the best method for evaluation. For one of our professional services clients, we came up with an alternative. Billable hours were important, but this client had a large amount of reoccurring revenue. They wanted to keep this reoccurring revenue. But billable hours did not capture this information.

We determined that the most important metric for their business was creating happy clients. Happy clients continued to do business with them. Happy clients gave them testimonials and referred business.

How can you quantify client happiness?

We created a metric called Happy Client. Happy Client was meant to ensure that their clients were happy with their staff and services. It was comprised of three components:

1. Clients continue to use their services
2. No complaints
3. Collections were within reasonable payment terms

The Happy Clients metric was weighted on a client-by-client and employee-by-employee basis. For example, assume Employee A does 80 percent of the work for Client X and Employee B does 20 percent of the work. If Client X continues to use their service, does not complain, and pays their bills on time, Employee A will get the majority of the credit for Client X's satisfaction. Conversely, if Client X stops hiring us, complains about our service, and/or stops paying, Employee A will get most of the blame. Employee B will get a reduced amount of credit or blame in the above example.

Sounds complicated? It is! However, it actually became relatively simple once we developed the process for tracking and reporting the information. It is also important to note that the Happy Clients metric is not perfect. Sometime a business just can't pay its bills (e.g., bankruptcy). Sometimes a personality conflict will cause a client to discontinue services. Sometimes a complaint has nothing to do with an individual's performance. However, the idea is that the employees will be more proactive in identifying and resolving these types of issues.

Quantifiable

Regardless of what you pick, you must be able to quantify the activity with some form of number. This can be very simple (e.g., sales) or very difficult (e.g., administrative assistant activities). The important thing is being able to measure the metric with some form of number. Later in this chapter we give numerous examples for all areas of business.

Controllable

The employee has to be able to control the outcome. Making people responsible for outcomes they have no control over will actually reduce results, which is the exact opposite of the desired effect. This can cause an interesting dilemma in certain circumstances. For example, if your industry as a whole is down 20 percent this year, is it fair to hold your salesperson accountable for 10 percent growth this year? In my mind, the answer is yes. Results matter. A good salesperson will succeed in any market. Otherwise you will need to subsidize his or her failures (more on this later).

Ren J. Carlton, CPA, CSMC

At the professional services business we discussed previously, we used the Happy Clients metric to manage 80 percent of the staff. Although Happy Clients is the business's #1 success factor, some of their employees have little to no client interaction (e.g., controller, HR manager). Since they have no control over making their clients happy, it would be unfair to hold them accountable to this metric.

Step 2: Set Targets

Everyone has a set of numbers. Start with the top and work your way down. For example, if you have a sales goal of $5 million for the year, one of the metrics for your head of sales should be sales of $5 million. If he or she has a staff of five people, each of them may have a sales metric of $1 million each. The overall goals start at the top, and the subordinate team members must be responsible for their individual goals.

It is critical for your employees to commit to their goals. It is one thing to set expectations, it is another for someone committing to meet (or exceed) those expectations. The best way to accomplish this is through communication. I start the target-setting process by asking each employee what he or she believes is a fair goal for each metric. Often you will see employees set stricter metrics for themselves then you would set for them! This is OK, but the metrics also need to be realistic.

For example, let's assume your top salesperson says he is going to sell $3 million next year. Based on your available data, you expect him to generate closer to $2 million in sales. First you should discuss your concerns. Then you might create a stretch goal of $3 million (with the applicable awards). However, you should probably set the salesperson's actual goal closer to $2 million. This may seem counter-intuitive. After all, wouldn't $3 million in sales be great? The problem is you are likely setting your salesperson up for failure. In addition, how can you budget for $3 million in sales when you know it is extremely unlikely? Accuracy is especially important when setting sales goals, since it is typically less expensive to underestimate sales than it is to overestimate sales.

Step 3: Communicate Results

In the above example, we used a simple template we created in a spreadsheet program. Although we have searched, we have been unsuccessful in finding a software program that works better than our simple templates. The faster you can report the metrics the better. You do not want your employees seeing their March results in October. You want to give your employees sufficient time to correct their actions in time for the following report. Weekly scorecards should take no more than three days after the end of the reporting period, while monthly/quarterly/annual scorecards should take no more than fifteen days after the end of the reporting period.

Step 4: Manage Employees to Metrics

Now it is time to hold your employees accountable for their performance. Utilizing employee scorecards is a purely objective method for evaluating your team's performance. Reviews, bonuses, raises, promotions, and terminations should be relatively straightforward. Scorecards also give you an objective method to evaluate the contribution of employees that are more than just employees (e.g., family, friends, stakeholders).

Realize accountability can mean different things in different situations. In one of my examples above, the salesperson in the industry that is down 20 percent is expected to grow his sales by 10 percent. But what if he fails? Then it is decision time. The most obvious repercussion is a reduction/elimination of bonuses and or commissions (which is the nice thing about incentive-based compensation plans). But what if the industry is up and he still does not hit his numbers? What if he never hits his numbers? Should you fire him (after all, he is a great guy)? Assuming the goals were fair, you may need to take more severe corrective actions. This can include additional training, coaching, additional support, termination, etc. Obviously you need to get the whole story first. But if your employee is not performing, who is subsidizing that failure?

Realize that the right kind of employees will not be comfortable missing their numbers. That discomfort is good. Let it sting for at least a little while, then ask them why they were unable to hit their numbers. You will likely be surprised with the responses. Then you can address the issues, modify the goals, or deal with the individual. I have a client that actually makes excuses for his senior management team for not hitting their numbers (before they even have a chance to explain)! I'm not saying you never let them off the hook, but at least see what they have to say first. Discomfort can be a strong motivational tool.

Examples of Particular Areas

In the majority of the above examples, I used sales because it is easy. What about the other areas of your business? Depending on the specific area, it can get a bit tricky. Here are some examples:

1. CEO
   a. Market share
   b. Sales
   c. Growth
   d. Profitability
   e. Return on Investment (ROI)
2. Sales
   a. Total Sales: Dollar value of sales, quantity ordered, quantity of sales orders, and/or number of customers (per year, quarter, month, etc.)
   b. Sales from New Clients: Dollar value of sales, quantity ordered, quantity of sales orders, and/or number of customers (per year, quarter, month, etc.)
   c. Reoccurring Sales from Existing Clients: Dollar value of sales, quantity ordered, quantity of sales orders, and/or number of customers (per year, quarter, month, etc.)
   d. Gross Profit on Sales: Dollar value and/or percentage
   e. Telemarketing Calls Made: Per week, day, hour, etc.

f. Appointments Scheduled: Per month, week, day, etc.
g. Appointments Completed: Per month, week, day, etc.
h. Proposals Sent: Per month, week, day, etc.
i. Closing Percentage
   i. Total sales, sales from new clients, reoccurring sales from existing clients (numerator)
   ii. Appointments scheduled, appointments completed, proposals sent (denominator)
   iii. Examples: Number of customers/appointments completed, quantity of sales orders/appointments completed, etc.)

3. Operations
  a. Manufacturing
    i. Units Produced:
      1. By employee, shift, division, company (numerator)
      2. Per month, week, day, etc. (denominator)
      3. Examples: Employee/month, division/day, etc.
    ii. Rework: Per month, week, day, etc.
    iii. Scrap: Per month, week, day, etc.
  b. Inventory Management
    i. Inventory Turns: Cost of goods sold/average inventory, number of units sold/average number of inventory units, etc.
    ii. Inventory Levels: Dollar amount, quantity of units, etc.
    iii. Inventory Obsolescence: Dollar amount, quantity of units, etc.
  c. Billable hours
    i. By employee, shift, division, company (numerator)
    ii. Per month, week, day, etc. (denominator)
    iii. Examples: Employee/month, division/day, etc.
  d. Gross Profit: Dollar value and/or percentage
  e. Customer Complaints: Per month, week, day, etc.
  f. Happy Clients (defined earlier in this chapter): Clients continue to use services, no complaints, collections within reasonable payment terms
  g. Budgetary Goals: Actual expenses vs. budgeted expenditures

Ren J. Carlton, CPA, CSMC

4. Finance
    a. Timing of Reporting: Date delivered vs. date due
    b. Accuracy of Reporting: Amount of errors detected
    c. Accounts Receivable: Dollar amount or percentage overdue (this is used to monitor collection performance)
    d. Interest Expense: Budget vs. actual (this is used to monitor cash management performance)
    e. Audit Success: Taxation authority, outside CPA, etc.
    f. Outside CPA Fees: Used to monitor internal finance team's performance
    g. Financing: Bank, private equity, etc.
    h. Budgetary Goals: Actual expenses vs. budgeted expenditures

5. HR
    a. Employee Turnover: Number of terminated and departing employees/average amount of employees (per year, quarter, month, etc.)
    b. Speed of Hiring: Number of days from decision to hire to actual hire date
    c. Timely Reviews: Date completed vs. date due
    d. Employee Complaints: Per year, quarter, month, etc.
    e. Employment Lawsuits: Per year, quarter, month, etc.
    f. Budgetary Goals: Actual expenses vs. budgeted expenditures
    g. Ratio of Filled Positions/Vacant Positions
    h. Percentage of Internal/Referral Hires

6. IT
    a. Downtime: Per quarter, month, week, etc.
    b. Outside IT Support Expenses: Actual expenses vs. budgeted expenditures
    c. Budgetary Goals: Actual expenses vs. budgeted expenditures

7. Administrative
    a. Completion of Assigned Tasks
    b. Percentage of Deadlines Met
    c. Amount of Calls Going to Voicemail: Per day, week, etc.
    d. Office Appearance: Cleanliness, organization, etc.

  e. Support Performance: Metrics measuring assistance in other areas (e.g., sales, operation)
  f. Budgetary Goals: Actual expenses vs. budgeted expenditures
8. Instructor
  a. Percentage of Satisfied Attendees
  b. Cost Per Attendee
  c. Instructor to Attendee Ratio
  d. Percentage Increase in Attendees
9. Project Manager
  a. Percentage of Quality Complaints
  b. Ratio of Successful Projects Compared to Total Projects Assigned
  c. Number of Conflicts
10. Maintenance
  a. Percent Rise in Maintenance Costs
  b. Number of Office Quality Standards Met
  c. Effectiveness of Maintenance Workforce
11. Medical
  a. Patient Satisfaction Ratings
  b. Cases of Negligence
  c. Patient of Out-Care Revenue
  d. Average Length of Stay
  e. Cost of Treatment
12. Hotel Manager
  a. Profit Per Room
  b. Ratio of Positive Feedback Vs. Negative Feedback
  c. Amount of Rooms Booked Directly Vs. Through Agencies
  d. Room Occupancy

Objective Performance Results

Assuming you are setting reasonable metrics, you now have a fair methodology for evaluating your team's performance. You essentially no longer need to be the bad guy as the numbers can dictate your course of action. I have a friend/client that has a unique approach to employee scorecards. He produces metrics for all of his employees based on his budget. He writes everyone's metrics on a large whiteboard in the middle of the office. This whiteboard shows everyone's targets and actual results. When he hires someone, he shows him or her the board and explains that he doesn't fire anyone. The board fires non-performing employees based on their numbers. During termination meetings, there are no surprises. Everyone knows what is expected and what the results are. How much clearer can you be with your performance reviews?

Action Items

1. Identify the employee activities that create value for your business
2. Create an employee scorecard for every employee of your business
3. Report employee scorecards on a monthly basis

CHAPTER 5: COOKING THE BOOKS – HELPING YOUR BUSINESS SHINE

"Where all the women are strong, all the men are good looking, and all the children are above average." Quote describing the fictional location Lake Wobegon

A businessman was interviewing applicants for the position of divisional manager. He devised a test to select the most suitable person for the job. He asked each applicant the question, "What is two plus two?" The first interviewee was a mathematician. His answer was "Four." The second applicant was an engineer. He pulled out his slide rule and showed his answer to be between 3.999 and 4.001. The last applicant was an accountant. When the businessman asked him the question, the accountant got up from his chair and closed the blinds. Then he closed the door and came back to sit down. He leaned across the desk and said in a low voice, "How much do you want it to be?" Author Unknown

Chapter Highlights
1. When cooking the books is appropriate
2. When you should consider deviating from Generally Accepted Accounting Principles (GAAP)
3. Methods for manipulating your financial data

I debated about including this chapter in the book. Although it is not my intention, the information in this chapter can be abused. I ultimately decided that legally cooking the books is a critical skill for attracting investors and lenders, as well as satisfying the occasional customer or vendor requests.

What Does Cooking the Books Mean?

Cooking the Books (also known as creative accounting and earnings management) are euphemisms referring to accounting practices that may follow the letter of the rules of standard accounting practices, but certainly deviate from the spirit of those rules. They

are characterized by excessive complication and the use of novel ways of characterizing income, assets, or liabilities and the intent to influence readers toward the interpretations desired by the authors. The terms "innovative" or "aggressive" are also sometimes used. The term as generally understood refers to systematic misrepresentation of the true income and assets of corporations or other organizations. "Creative accounting" is at the root of a number of accounting scandals, and many proposals for accounting reform—usually centering on an updated analysis of capital and factors of production that would correctly reflect how value is added. Wikipedia

When the Bottom Line Isn't the Bottom Line

For almost every business, the owner can produce an income statement and balance sheet. This set of financial statements may only be prepared for tax purposes, but most entrepreneurs understand the need for this information (albeit maybe only on an annual basis). Since these statements are the most commonly produced, they are also the most viewed. The problem is that these statements only show a limited amount of information.

An Income Statement, also called a Profit and Loss Statement (P&L), is a financial statement for companies that indicates how Revenue (money received from the sale of products and services before expenses are taken out, also known as the "top line") is transformed into net income (the result after all revenues and expenses have been accounted for, also known as the "bottom line"). The purpose of the income statement is to show managers and investors whether the company made or lost money during the period being reported. The important thing to remember about an income statement is that it represents a period of time. This contrasts the balance sheet, which represents a single moment in time. Wikipedia

A balance sheet or statement of financial position is a summary of a person's or organization's balances. Assets, liabilities, and ownership equity are listed as of a specific date, such as the end of its

financial year. A balance sheet is often described as a snapshot of a company's financial condition. The balance sheet is the only statement which applies to a single point in time. A company balance sheet has three parts: assets, liabilities, and shareholders' equity. The main categories of assets are usually listed first and are followed by the liabilities. The difference between the assets and the liabilities is known as equity or the net assets or the net worth of the company; according to the accounting equation, net worth must equal assets minus liabilities. Wikipedia

Although these statements are critical for understanding the financial condition of your business, they do not tell the whole story. The problem is most businesses only utilize these two statements. This is fine when talking to insiders of the business, but what happens when you are talking to investors or lenders? It helps to produce supplemental management reports, but even these can fall short of telling the true story. The goal of this chapter is to teach you how to modify the rules in order for you to accurately portray your business to outsiders.

Taxes

Everything I suggest in this chapter is perfectly legal; however, the techniques I discuss may not be proper for tax return preparation purposes. There are strict federal, state, and local reporting requirements associated with preparing your tax returns. That being said, the techniques discussed in this chapter are typically designed to increase the income and assets you report. The goal for most people is to minimize their income for tax return reporting purposes, since a large portion of business taxes are based on income. That being said, you could essentially do the opposite I am describing to reduce your income (and therefore reduce income-based taxes). I highly recommend you consult your CPA before utilizing any of the techniques I describe for tax return preparation purposes.

Ideally, you should have two sets of books (or at least two sets of financial statements). The financial statements you use for lenders, investors, etc. that maximize income (referred to as "book" or "book purposes"), with another set of financial statements for income tax return purposes that minimizes income (referred to as "tax" or "tax purposes"). Going forward, we will spend a great deal of time discussing book-to-tax differences. Although you need to follow certain guidelines, keeping two (or more) sets of books can be perfectly legal.

Assets and Expenses

Let's assume you wrote a check for $1,000 to Vendor Inc. We will also assume you are using cash-basis accounting. How does this cash outflow show up on your books? Generally speaking, you can either book the payment as an expense to your business or an asset to your business. If you post the $1,000 outflow as an expense, it reduces your net income by $1,000. However, if you post the $1,000 as an asset there is no impact to net income.

So one way to improve the bottom line is to capitalize expenses (record an expense as an asset) or understate liabilities (record a liability as revenue). Let's say you spent $30,000 on software. As of the writing of this book, many businesses can utilize a $30,000 tax deduction for this software purchase (which is good). However, your financial statements will also show this $30,000 expense. This will cause a $30,000 reduction in income (which is bad).

An alternative is to capitalize the $30,000 cash outlay as an asset. Although you will be required to depreciate the asset (expense the expenditure in small increments over the life of the asset), your bottom line will still be much better (relative to expensing the entire asset at the time of purchase). The only drawback is you may postpone some of your $30,000 tax deduction. The ideal scenario is to expense the entire $30,000 for tax purposes but capitalize the entire $30,000 for book purposes. Maintaining two sets of books enables you to utilize this strategy.

Software is pretty easy to identify as a potential asset to capitalize. But what about something that is a bit more creative? For example, what if you invested in a large branding campaign for your company? Isn't that creating a form of asset? After all, branding can offer years of benefit to your business. This benefit can last well beyond the date you write the checks to pay for it. Should the entire expense be recognized in the month or year you wrote the checks? Here are some other examples that may justify capitalization:

1. Opening a satellite office
2. Costs of writing a business plan
3. Employee costs associated with the time spent renovating your building

Be creative. In my mind, anything that has a useful life is fair game.

Revenues and Liabilities

The relationship between revenues and liabilities is similar to the relationship between assets and expenses; the difference is assets/expenses are debit accounts, revenues/expenses are credit accounts. Let's assume you received a check for $1,000 from Customer Inc. How does this cash inflow show up on your books? Generally speaking, you can either record this $1,000 cash receipt as revenue or as a liability. If you post the $1,000 inflow of cash as revenue, it increases your net income by $1,000. However, if you post the $1,000 as a liability there is no impact on the bottom line (net income).

If the $1,000 represents a deposit from Customer Inc., the cash receipt is technically a liability for accounting purposes. Since the work is not yet complete, you may need to refund the money. The money is not earned—which is why "unearned revenue" is a name commonly used for the liability account used for this type of transaction. But what if you receive a non-refundable deposit from a customer? If you are using accrual-based accounting, you still book the deposit as a liability, primarily due to the matching principle, which will be discussed later in this chapter. Is that proper?

Shouldn't you be able to book at least some of that cash as revenue, boosting sales and net income?

In an ideal world, every cash outlay would be used to purchase assets and every cash inflow would generate revenue for your financial statement reporting purposes (e.g., book purposes). Conversely, you want every cash outlay to incur an expense (e.g., be tax deductible) and treat every cash inflow as a liability when calculating your income-based taxes (e.g., tax purposes). How can you accomplish this effectively (and legally)?

Generally Accepted Accounting Principles (GAAP)

U.S. financial statements are governed by Generally Accepted Accounting Principles (GAAP). This set of principles dictates rules for bookkeeping and financial statement presentation. The principles provide guidance regarding what you expense, what you capitalize, what you treat as revenue, etc. Generally speaking, most other countries have relatively similar guidelines and standards. Below are the basic accounting principles as dictated by GAAP:

1. **Economic Entity Assumption**: The accountant keeps all of the business transactions of a business entity separate from the stakeholders.
2. **Monetary Unit Assumption**: Economic activity is measured in dollars, and only transactions that can be expressed in dollars are recorded.
3. **Time Period Assumption**: This accounting principle assumes that it is possible to report business activities in distinct time intervals.
4. **Cost Principle**: The amounts shown on financial statements are reported at their historical cost amounts. Historical cost refers to the amount of cash or cash equivalent when an item was originally obtained.
5. **Full Disclosure Principle**: All relevant information regarding the financial condition (current and future) should be disclosed.

6. **Going Concern Principle:** Assumption that a company will continue to exist for the foreseeable future.

7. **Matching Principle:** Expenses need to be reported in the same period as the associated revenue generated by those expenses.

8. **Revenue Recognition Principle:** Revenues are recorded as soon as a product has been sold or a service has been performed, regardless of when the corresponding money is actually received.

9. **Materiality:** Amounts that are considered insignificant or immaterial may be ignored or reported inaccurately.

10. **Conservatism:** Reporting financial information in a manner that does not overstate income and/or assets.

As you will learn throughout this chapter, there are times when it makes sense to ignore some of these principles when producing financial information regarding your business.

Risks When Deviating from GAAP

Before you produce financial statements or management reports that deviate from GAAP, you need to consider the potential risk. An end-user of your financial statements may feel that you were being dishonest when you provided non-GAAP financial reports—especially if your GAAP-compliant financial statements are significantly different. You also may inadvertently expose yourself and your company to liability. It is typically assumed that any financial information you produce complies with the applicable accounting standards (in the U.S. this would be compliant with GAAP). Therefore, it is important to either disclose your failure to comply with GAAP or restrict the intended audience of your financial information. My preference is to restrict the intended audience through the inclusion of a simple disclosure.

We type "For Management Use Only" on all non-GAAP financial statements and management reports. This tells the readers that the information found on the sheet of paper is intended to be used by management only (even if they are viewed by a third party). This disclosure is designed to alleviate any liability caused by a third party relying on the underlying financial statement or management report. Since the disclosure identifies the end-user as management, you are not required to comply with GAAP. It is my firm's practice to include this disclosure whenever we take a financial position that deviates from GAAP. We also make sure we include this disclosure on every page of any report or statement we produce. You never know which third party may be viewing (and possibly relying) on the information you produce.

Limitations of Generally Accepted Accounting Principles (GAAP)

Although GAAP is mandatory in SOME circumstances, these principles often present businesses in a manner that understates the value or economic condition of a business. Here are some examples where it makes sense to consider deviating from GAAP in order to show your company's true strength.

1. **Economic Entity Assumption:** This assumption is flawed when there is a group of related businesses under the control of the same management team. Even though these related businesses may be separate legal entities with a variety of different owners, the businesses are essentially one large conglomerate.
2. **Monetary Unit Assumption:** Sometime it is difficult, if not expressly forbidden, to present the market value of certain assets on your financial statements (e.g., customer lists, marketing brand, employee retention). This can make your business appear to be less valuable than it is.
3. **Time Period Assumption:** This assumption can prohibit demonstrating the value of assets that have a long-term impact (e.g., marketing costs, websites). Again, this can be detrimental to the stated value of your business.
4. **Cost Principle:** This principle often prevents you from presenting your assets at their true market value (e.g., fully depreciated equipment that is still in use). This is especially true for assets that may appreciate (e.g., real estate). Inability to show the true value of your business assets understates the business's value.

5. **Full Disclosure Principle:** This principle can force businesses to disclose information that may scare away investors or lenders. These disclosures often ignore the likelihood that the disclosed events will actually occur.

6. **Going Concern Principle:** Telling the world that the business may not be around next year can be a self-fulfilling prophesy. Disclosing the fact that your business may not last another year is likely to scare away investors or financing source that may otherwise have supplied the needed capital for the business to survive.

7. **Matching Principle:** This principle can force a business to overstate expenses. This occurs when a business is forced to report business expenses that will generate additional revenue in the future (e.g., marketing costs, website development).

8. **Revenue Recognition Principle:** This principle prevents you from showing revenue from work you have not yet completed, even if the revenue is guaranteed and you have already been paid.

9. **Materiality:** Although this is a favorable principle, it is somewhat vague. Expanding the principle often makes sense when you want to omit material information, especially when it is irrelevant to future performance.

10. **Conservatism:** This principle stops you from booking items that are extremely likely but not guaranteed (e.g., proceeds from a lawsuit your business will likely win).

When you produce your non-GAAP financial information, you have the freedom to modify these principles to properly reflect the economic condition of your business. For example, we have a client that owns a large number of travel agencies. When my client sells a vacation package, my client receives a deposit that is non-refundable (even if the trip never occurs). Per GAAP, this revenue should not be recognized until after the trip occurs (Revenue Recognition Principle). In our opinion, this principle would cause my client to understate sales. My client has absolutely no responsibility for the trip. The only obligation of my client is booking the underlying flights, hotels, etc. Since my client does this at the point of sale, we produced income statements that show the revenue of vacations earned when paid (with the "Management Use Only" disclosure).

Whether you are looking to boost your business's income or net worth, there are numerous methods available. With a little bit of creativity you can modify your reporting in order to accomplish a wide variety of desired results (without committing fraud). It is important for you to have a reasonable argument for your position, in addition to consistent application of your position throughout your statements.

Financial Data Manipulation

Here is a list of methods for manipulating financial data. Although the list is far from exhaustive, it provides a number of areas you can modify to help accurately portray your business:

1. Acceleration of Revenue Recognition
2. Deferral of Expenses
3. Related Party Transactions
4. Cash Basis Reporting
5. Stakeholder Loans vs. Compensation
6. Balance Sheet Presentation
7. Income Statement Presentation
8. Prior Period Adjustments

Acceleration of Revenue Recognition

One way to improve your income and balance sheet is to accelerate the recognition of revenue. This tactic is used to recognize revenue before it is considered earned by GAAP standards. Methods for accelerating revenue include recognizing sales that are not yet earned or complete. Another method is to book sales that are actually earned in another period (e.g., recognizing January 2010 sales on your 2009 income statement). Flagrant abuse of the Revenue Recognition Principle includes backdating sales and fabricating fictitious sales.

Deferral of Expenses

Another way to improve your income and balance sheet is to defer expenses, despite what the Matching Principle dictates. Tactics include postponing the posting of current expenses until future periods (e.g., recognizing 2009 expenses in January 2010). You can also capitalize transactions that may not have a useful life according to GAAP (e.g., certain marketing costs). Flagrant abuse of the Matching Principle includes failing to post expenses and counting inventory that is no longer owned by the company, which understates expenses by understating cost of goods sold.

Related Party Transactions

Related party transactions are purchases and sales between companies under common control. Although this relationship may not be considered a related party (or control group) legally, I am referring to situations where one set of managers controls the books of two or more companies. The manipulation occurs when a favorable transaction happens only on one set of books in a related party transaction.

For example, let's assume Company A sells Company B $100,000 worth of product. For illustrative purposes, let's also assume that A had $0 costs associated with this sale. If you consolidate the activity of these two entities for reporting purposes (combining the books of Company A and Company B to show one income statement, one balance sheet, etc.), what is the net income result? There is none. Company A had a $100,000 sale, Company B had a $100,000 expense, and this transaction has a net income effect of $0.

$100,000 Revenue - $100,000 Expense = $0 Net Income

If you are only reporting Company A's performance, you just improved the bottom line by $100,000! Conversely, you decreased Company B's individual performance by $100,000.

What happens if only Company A books the transaction? If you consolidate the activity of these two entities for reporting purposes, what is the net income result? Again, there is a $100,000 increase in net income. Company A had a $100,000 sale, company B had no expense. This results in a net income effect of $100,000 (albeit inaccurately).

$100,000 Revenue - $0 Expense = $100,000 Net Income

These are just a couple of examples of how intercompany transactions can be controlled to produce a wide variety of results.

Cash Basis Reporting

Although cash is king, accrual basis is critical in obtaining a true picture of your business performance. It illustrates what revenue you have earned and what expenses you owe. Accrual basis also differentiates between assets and expenses, as well as revenue and liabilities. For this reason, the majority of lenders and stakeholders require accrual-basis statements.

For most businesses it is ideal to have accrual-based financial statements and management reports, with cash-basis tax reporting. Accrual-basis accounting records financial events based on economic activity rather than financial activity. Under accrual accounting, revenue is recorded when it is earned and realized, regardless of when actual payment is received. Similarly, expenses are matched to revenue regardless of when they are actually paid.

Cash-basis accounting is a method of bookkeeping that records financial events based on cash flows and cash position. Revenue is recognized when cash is received and expense is recognized when cash is paid. Although accrual basis is important for understanding the true financial condition of your business, you don't always want to share that level of detail with every audience. Certain circumstances require only a limited amount of information.

In those cases, you may want to consider providing cash-basis information.

Stakeholder Loans vs. Compensation

When cash flow is tight, working stakeholders may forego compensation in order to preserve cash. When earnings are tight, it sometimes also makes sense to reduce or eliminate stakeholder compensation. Occasionally there are situations where cash is abundant but earnings are tight. In those circumstances, it may make sense for the shareholder to take loans from the company versus traditional compensation. Loans are typically tax-free and have no impact on net income—other than the applicable interest on the loans. Sure, the stakeholder eventually must pay the loans back (or convert the loans to compensation and pay the applicable payroll taxes), but this can be a short-term remedy for producing positive earnings. It is also important to consult with your tax advisor before utilizing this tactic; there are interest rate and documentation requirements associated with stakeholder loans.

Balance Sheet Presentation

Most people confuse a balance sheet with a statement of net worth. It is easy to do, because they are very similar. However, does equity (which is reported on the balance sheet) truly reflect worth? Illustration C-1 shows a typical balance sheet.

Ren J. Carlton, CPA, CSMC

```
                              Growth Inc.
                             Balance Sheet
                             April 30th, 2010


    Current Assets
        Cash                                        $        2,555,268
        Accounts Receivable                                  1,539,981
        Inventory                                            1,167,142
        Prepaid Expenses                                       152,511
        Notes Receivable                                     4,608,709
            Total Current Assets                            10,023,611
    Fixed Assets
        Machinery & Equipment                                2,525,217
        Furniture & Fixtures                                   619,645
        Less: Accumulated Depreciation                      (1,711,665)
            Total Assets                            $       11,456,808


    Current Liabilities
        Accounts Payable                                     1,635,164
        Wages Payable                                          148,783
        Taxes Payable                                          19,548
        Other Expenses Payable                               1,260,953
            Total Current Liabilities                        3,064,448


    Bonds Payable                                            1,500,000
            Total Liabilities                                4,564,448


    Equity and Earnings
        Common Stock                                          402,000
        Retained Earnings                                    5,350,155
        Dividends Paid                                      (1,900,000)
        Accumulated Net Income                               3,040,205
            Total Equity & Earnings                          6,892,360
            Total Liabilities & Equity              $       11,456,808


                          For Management Use Only                    C-1
```

Generally speaking, the balance sheet shows line items at historical cost. A traditional balance sheet understates the value of depreciated assets that hold their value. For example, let's assume you own a press that was originally purchased seven years ago for $1.5 million. More than likely this piece of equipment is fully depreciated on your books. Assuming this is the case, your press would be shown as an asset with $0 value on your balance sheet:

Equipment (reported at cost): $ 1,500,000
Less Accumulated Depreciation: 1,500,000
Fixed Assets (as reported on the balance sheet): $ 0

Let's assume your press is still worth approximately $600,000. Where is this $600,000 asset value presented on your financial statements? The answer is it isn't. This can have a substantial impact on your books. Even though equity is not truly net worth, many people think of it that way. This methodology clarifies the value of the business. Assets we tend to revalue include property, buildings, equipment, inventory, and certain intangible assets (patents, trademarks, etc.). My firm almost always prepares this report when helping a client obtain financing. Due to the Historical Cost and Conservative Principle, net worth is almost always greater than equity. Illustration C-2 shows a statement of net worth. Notice the net worth reported on Illustration C-2 far exceeds the Total Equity & Earnings reported on Illustration C-1.

Growth Inc.
Statement of Net Worth
April 30th, 2010

Current Assets		
Cash	$	2,555,268
Accounts Receivable		1,539,981
Inventory		1,500,000
Prepaid Expenses		152,511
Notes Receivable		4,608,709
Total Current Assets		10,356,469
Fixed Assets		
Machinery & Equipment		2,500,000
Furniture & Fixtures		700,000
Total Assets	$	**13,556,469**
Current Liabilities		
Accounts Payable		1,635,164
Wages Payable		148,783
Taxes Payable		19,548
Other Expenses Payable		1,260,953
Total Current Liabilities		3,064,448
Notes Payable		1,500,000
Total Liabilities		4,564,448
Net Worth	$	**8,992,021**

For Management Use Only   C-2

Income Statement Presentation

We use a couple of methods to improve the appearance of net income. The first is producing a normalized income statement. This is a pro-forma statement that shows what the net income should have looked like over the past period. We simply modify the revenue and expense accounts to show what would likely have happened if some unforeseen events did not occur (e.g., increase in costs, termination of a top salesperson).

The second method we use is categorizing unusual expense items in an "Extraordinary Items" section of the income statement. Although this does not alter income, it does show what income would look like if these extraordinary items did not exist. They can include one-time charges (e.g., marketing initiatives, expansion/divestiture costs), legal fees associated with a resolved lawsuit, etc. Anything that is outside of the ordinary course of your business can be considered for this section. Illustration C-3 shows a typical income statement before the categorization of unusual expenses, whereas Illustration C-4 shows the income statement after the categorization. Even though net income is the same, Illustration C-4 highlights the fact that the business would have been much more profitable without the extraordinary items.

Growth Inc.
Income Statement
For the Month Ending, April 30th, 2010

Revenue:	$	1,495,948
Cost of Goods Sold:		
Materials		400,157
Freight		134,265
Labor		230,112
Total Cost of Goods Sold		764,534
Gross Profit		731,414
Selling, Gen., and Admin. Expenses		
Payroll		195,642
Bad Debts		9,500
Travel		407
Dues & Subscriptions		3,381
Legal & Professional		35,540
Utilities		18,163
Telephone		8,262
Rent		120,000
Postage		5,541
General Insurance		5,200
Worker's Compensation Insurance		6,000
Employee Health Insurance		34,488
Property Tax		12,659
State Income Tax		25,000
Payroll Processing		2,566
Office Supplies		7,206
Fuel		4,048
Depreciation		64,000
Miscellaneous		(108)
Total Selling, Gen., and Admin. Expense		557,495
Net Income	**$**	**173,919**

For Management Use Only   C-3

Ren J. Carlton, CPA, CSMC

Growth Inc.
Income Statement
For the Month Ended, April 30th, 2010

Revenue:	$	1,495,948
Cost of Goods Sold:		
Materials		350,157
Freight		134,265
Labor		155,112
Total Cost of Goods Sold		639,534
Gross Profit		856,414
Selling, Gen., and Admin. Expenses		
Payroll		144,548
Bad Debts		9,500
Travel		407
Dues & Subscriptions		3,381
Legal & Professional		35,540
Utilities		18,163
Telephone		8,262
Rent		120,000
Postage		5,541
General Insurance		5,200
Worker's Compensation Insurance		6,000
Employee Health Insurance		34,488
Property Tax		12,659
State Income Tax		25,000
Payroll Processing		2,566
Office Supplies		7,206
Fuel		4,048
Depreciation		64,000
Miscellaneous		(108)
Total Selling, Gen., and Admin. Expense		506,401
Income from Operations	**$**	**350,013**
Extraordinary Items		
Inventory loss from fire		50,000
Bonuses		126,094
Net Income	**$**	**173,919**

For Management Use Only   C-4

Prior Period Adjustments

There are often situations where you may be able to justify showing expenses as a prior period adjustment. Reasons for this treatment can include receiving bills late from expenses from the prior period, unforeseen liabilities that were created because of something that happened last year, recently discovered theft that impacted prior years, etc. These expenses reduce retained earnings directly, never adjusting the current period's net income. Although the balance sheet effect is identical, it improves the reported net income.

For example, let's assume Company A has $1,000,000 of sales and $1,150,000 of expenses. For illustrative purposes, let's assume the only balance sheet account is cash. The company would have a loss of $150,000:

$1,000,000 Revenue - $1,150,000 Expense = ($150,000) Net Loss

The balance sheet would look like this:

Assets

Cash:	$ 100,000
Total Assets:	$ 100,000

Liabilities and Equity

Total Liabilities:	$ 0

Equity
Prior Period Adjustment:	$ 0
Retained Earnings:	(150,000)
Common Stock:	250,000
Total Liabilities & Equity:	$ 100,000

Now let's assume everything stays the same, but the controller of Company A asserts that $250,000 of the expenses were associated with an event that occurred in the previous year. The company would now show net income of $100,000!

$1,000,000 Revenue - $900,000 Expense = $100,000 Net Income

The balance sheet would look like this:

Assets

Cash:	$ 100,000
Total Assets:	$ 100,000

Liabilities and Equity

Total Liabilities:	$ 0

Equity
Prior Period Adjustment:	$ (250,000)
Retained Earnings:	100,000
Common Stock:	250,000
Total Liabilities & Equity:	$ 100,000

Again, the balance sheet still shows the same equity. However, net income is significantly improved.

Action Items
1. Determine situations where your company would benefit from cooking the books
2. Identify Generally Accepted Accounting Principles (GAAP) that cause you to understate the value of your business
3. Determine which methods for manipulating your financial data is applicable to your company

CHAPTER 6: FINANCING – SECURING THE CASH YOUR BUSINESS NEEDS

"A bank is a place that will lend you money if you can prove you don't need it." Bob Hope

Chapter Highlights
1. How to overcome common financing challenges
2. What you should do before you approach a lender
3. Finding the financing source that is right for you and your business
4. What happens if you default

I would argue that running out of cash is the most common reason businesses fail, regardless of the size or industry of the company. Having sufficient cash reserves and financing availability is critical for both short- and long-term success.

In this chapter, I am going to focus the majority of my time discussing bank financing. Although we will address other options, banks are typically the simplest and cheapest way to obtain commercial financing. In addition, most lenders and private investors utilize some, if not all, of a bank's processes when evaluating financing opportunities. Although throughout this chapter I primarily use the term *bank*, in most circumstances you can substitute the terms *financing* or *investment source*.

The 5 Cs of Credit

The five elements lenders typically use in evaluating a potential lending opportunity are:
1. **Collateral:** Assets used to secure the debt. Since most lenders are considered asset-based lenders, they typically require assets that are convertible into cash. Examples include accounts receivable, inventory, equipment, buildings, and land.
2. **Capacity:** The ability to pay back the debt. History, past performance, and budgets demonstrate the capacity of

the business. A strong capacity can sometimes overcome businesses with insufficient collateral—which is often the case in service-based businesses and acquisition financing.

3. **Capital:** The net worth of the company. Generally speaking this comes down to the strength of the balance sheet. Personal guarantees can help establish sufficient capital for businesses lacking sufficient net worth.

4. **Conditions:** This includes the overall conditions of the business, the industry (both lending and business), and the overall economy. Unfortunately this element is often out of the business's control.

5. **Character:** The integrity of the business, owners, and management team. This element includes credit scores, reputation, and references. The strength of the management team also helps establish strong character.

Financing Challenges

Although none of these challenges is necessarily insurmountable by itself, here are common problems within each element:

1. **Collateral:** Insufficient bankable assets (assets that are somewhat easy to convert into cash). Service-based businesses, startups, and intellectual property companies often struggle with this issue. Questionable bankable assets can also cause a problem (e.g., inventory/equipment that is difficult to sell, uncollectable receivables).

2. **Capacity:** Businesses that have been incurring losses. Startups without a sufficient history of profitable performance.

3. **Capital:** Businesses with little (or possibly negative) net worth.

4. **Conditions:** Business transition, declining industry, or poor economy.

5. **Character:** Bad credit scores (business and/or owners) or weak management team.

Financing – Is it really worth it?

When I was in business school, I was under the delusion that entrepreneurs used other people's money to get rich. Now I would argue that this is the exception as opposed to the norm. When most of my friends and I started our businesses, we had very little financing. For me, it wasn't because I lacked potential sources of financing (credit cards). Rather it was because of a simple truth that seems to escape a large portion of the population. You are expected to pay loans back! Whether it is a legal requirement or a moral obligation, most lenders expect you to repay your debt at some point.

For me, entrepreneurship is about freedom and flexibility. The ability to do whatever you want, whenever you want to do it is awesome. Obviously this freedom and flexibility also gives you the freedom not to have any customers and the flexibility not to make any money! You have to take the good with the bad. The point being, debt inhibits this freedom and flexibility. I have a client that is essentially being forced to work for the bank. Their business was fully leveraged. Now they are in default with the bank. The bank wants their money back. My client doesn't have it. My client is helping the bank collect as much cash as possible before they close their doors. We hope the bank won't enforce the personal guarantees. Although my client still "owns" the "business," it doesn't feel very entrepreneurial to me.

Don't get me wrong, I understand that not every business has the luxury of avoiding outside financing. And sure, MAYBE you could accelerate your ten-year plan to five years. But ultimately you must evaluate whether debt is really worth it to you (e.g., personal guarantees, debt covenants, interest costs). In my opinion, there are only a few reasons to incur debt. These include:

1. **Working Capital:** Financing used to help manage the Cash Conversion Cycle (or Cash-to-Cash Cycle). This is financing the purchase of a widget today for the ability to sell it at a later date (hopefully for a profit). The proceeds

from these sales should be used to pay off the corresponding debt.

2. **Income-Producing Furniture, Equipment, Building, and Land:** Essentially anything you NEED in your business to make money. Income-producing means it will either increase revenue or decrease cost. The income generated from these purchases should be used to pay down the debt in a reasonable amount of time.

3. **Income-Producing Acquisitions:** Identifying situations where 1+1=3. When done properly, acquisitions should earn additional income through elimination of redundant headcount/overhead, cross-selling product/services, etc. Again, the income benefit generated from the acquisition should be used to pay down the debt in a reasonable amount of time.

All other costs should be funded by equity. This can be equity from your personal net worth, retained earnings, friends, family, or outside investors.

Assembling a Financing Package

If you determined that you need financing, you need to assemble a solid financing package BEFORE you approach the bank. Here are the documents we assemble when we prepare the initial financing package:

1. Company overview or summary, including:
   a. Business plan
   b. Description of products or services
   c. Management and executive team profiles
2. Budget for the next twelve months
3. Reason financing is needed and the applicable collateral
4. Most recent set of interim financial statements available (ideally no more than two months old), including an income statement, balance sheet, and net worth statement
5. Available appraisals for buildings and equipment

6. Prior year corporate tax returns – prior two years
7. Prior year financial statements – prior two years
8. Net worth statement of primary stakeholder(s) and estimated credit scores
9. Personal tax returns for stakeholders – prior two years

Story Time!

When you are looking for financing, a good story goes a long way (especially when you are trying to obtain financing for a less-than-perfect business). What has changed that is going to make the future better than the past? Who have you hired/fired? What have you learned? Although most financiers will not ignore the numbers entirely, a good story can make the difference when your business is a somewhat risky investment. When I say good story, I mean a story rooted in believable facts (e.g., solid projections, defendable assumptions, strong business plan). I have seen a good story make up for every one of The 5 Cs of Credit.

Picking the Correct Financing Option

We have a saying at our firm: right business, right lender (person), right bank (institution the lender represents). Your business needs to be bankable, your individual lender needs to believe in you and your business, and your bank has to support your business and industry. It is often a formula for disaster when these items are not aligned.

We had a client with a wonderful business and a great lender. Unfortunately the bank the lender represented no longer supported my client's industry (my client was a building contractor). My client was never able to get adequate financing, regardless of how hard their lender worked to get them additional financing. Eventually we helped our client find a bank and a lender that believed in my client's business and industry.

Ren J. Carlton, CPA, CSMC

Here are some of the criteria we consider when evaluating financing sources:
1. Philosophy
2. Stability
3. Lender quality
4. Bank mergers

Philosophy

All banks have an ideal client profile. Larger banks have multiple departments, each with a relatively unique ideal client profile. You need to make sure your business is as close to your bank's (or bank department's) ideal client profile as possible. Different banks target different company sizes, industries, geographic regions, etc.

Stability

We typically work with lenders that are financially strong and consistent. We like to see a proven track record and good reputation. You don't want to be involved with a lender that continuously changes its philosophy. Not too long ago, one of the larger U.S. banks made a strategic decision to exit middle-market lending. They pretty much got rid of the majority of the loans in this market (both good and not-so-good businesses). This caused a lot of turmoil for some of our clients, at no fault of their own. The funny thing is the same bank changed their philosophy again a few years later and re-entered middle market lending!

We also use caution when dealing with small lenders. Although some small banks are great, others are undercapitalized. When a bank is undercapitalized, it may not be capable of handling difficult times. In our experience, smaller banks tend to overreact when our clients do not perform as well as anticipated. Your bank needs to be able to stick with you through good and bad times.

Lender Quality

Again, you need to have the right lender on board. In an ideal situation, your lender will be your advocate to the bank. We interview lenders almost as thoroughly as employees. We also watch out for frequent lender turnover. This can be a sign of instability.

Bank Mergers

Banks merge frequently. What may have been an ideal situation for you yesterday may no longer apply after an acquisition. Change almost always occurs when your bank is the seller in a merger situation. Sometimes the transition may be slow, but the reality is that you are now reporting to a different master. It may be better, it may be worse, but it will definitely be different.

In an ideal world, you have three banks competing for your business (which is exactly the situation my firm tries to create when shopping financing for our clients). Unfortunately, underperforming businesses are rarely in that position. Struggling businesses are often lucky to attract a single interested lender, much less three. In those situations, you may need to take what you can get. That is fine for a short-term solution; however, you should always be searching for a lender and bank that is in alignment with your business.

Financing Options

Regardless of what you have read or heard, financing options are relatively limited for most entrepreneurs. Below are the most common financing sources available:

1. Owners and stakeholders
2. Friends and Family
3. Banks
4. SBA loans
5. Factoring and asset based lending
6. Mezzanine financing and subordinated debt
7. Private equity
8. Venture capital and angel investors
9. Grants
10. Vendors

Ren J. Carlton, CPA, CSMC

11. Customers
12. Competitors

Owners and Stakeholders

Like it or not, you and your partners are the most likely source for financing your business. For startups, you will likely finance 100 percent of the operation in the beginning. It is typically the only option available. The source of these funds include personal savings, retirement accounts (be careful of early withdraw consequences), second mortgages, personal line of credit, and credit cards. The structure can include debt or equity (ownership), and the terms are often negotiable (e.g., interest rate, payback terms, covenants).

Friends and Family

As with stakeholders, these types of funds are cheap and flexible. The major concern with accepting these funds is default risk. As a stakeholder, you should understand the risk of investing in a business. What happens if everything goes wrong and your business is unable to repay the loans to your parents? Will you be personally responsible to pay the loans back to a lifelong friend? If not, will these relationships survive? I suggest a very candid discussion before entering into related-party financing. I also recommend using an attorney to draft the documents. If things do go bad and the relationship is ruined, the legal documents can add clarity to an already unpleasant situation.

Banks

Bank financing is the most readily accessible, non-relationship financing option available. It is also one of the cheapest. The only catch is your business must be bankable—or strong enough to merit financing. Banks will perform due diligence to validate your financial information (which you will pay for). In addition, banks always require interest and will frequently monitor the health of your business via loan covenants. If you are unable to maintain the health of your business—by failing to hit the benchmarks set forth in your loan covenants—the bank can force you into default, even if you do not miss a single payment. Even with these issues, the bank is frequently a business's most viable option.

SBA Loans

Small Business Administration (SBA) loans are bank loans that are at least partially guaranteed by the federal government. The loan is still with a bank; however, the U.S. government will pay the bank back some of the money if you and your business default on the loan. This guaranty helps banks lend money to businesses that do not meet the bank's normal credit standards. These types of loans are more expensive, but they are often the only available option for some businesses (e.g., startups, businesses with performance challenges). The specific programs vary and are constantly changing. For more information, contact your bank. Even though all larger banks participate in the SBA program, some banks are better than others. Make sure you do your homework.

Factoring and Asset-Based Lending

Sometimes an SBA guaranty is not enough. When businesses are already in financial trouble, it can be tough to find a bank to lend you money, even with an SBA guaranty. In those circumstances, there are alternatives. Assuming you have business assets with value, you may want to consider factoring and asset-based lending. Factoring companies purchase your accounts receivable. Asset-based lenders finance equipment, inventory, and real estate.

There are two potential problems with this type of financing: advance rate and cost. The advance rate for this type of financing is typically much less than the underlying asset. For example, assume you have a piece of equipment worth $250,000. If you were able to find an asset-based lender to offer you financing, the advance rate may be as low as 50 percent, meaning they would lend you $125,000.

Ren J. Carlton, CPA, CSMC

The second problem is cost. This type of money is typically extremely expensive. In one client situation, the due diligence costs, maintenance costs, points, and interest rate added up to an annual effective interest rate of over 30 percent! Before you take this kind of money, make sure your margins are good enough to support this expense.

Mezzanine Financing and Subordinated Debt

When medium-sized businesses (businesses with annual sales over $10 million and annual EBITDA over $1 million) need financing, mezzanine financing and subordinated debt becomes an option. This type of debt is secondary to the primary lender. If the business were to liquidate, the primary lender (typically the bank) would get paid off before the secondary lender. If all of the assets are gone and no money is left, the secondary lender gets nothing. This type of financing varies in structure and terms. It may not require interest payments immediately, it may require equity, and the provider may become active in the management of the business. This type of financing is designed to provide expansion capital or help stakeholders reduce their investment in their business.

Private Equity

Private equity is another form of financing that is designed for medium-sized businesses (except for venture capital, which is discussed later in this chapter). Although some of the funds may be structured as debt, the majority of the funds you receive will be used to purchase an ownership stake in your company. In this case, the private equity investor almost always takes some form of active role in the management of the business (e.g., senior management position(s), role(s) on the board of directors).

Venture Capital and Angel Investors

Venture capital and angel investors are individuals/groups that invest cash in exchange for equity. There are two major issues with these types of funds. The first is availability. Unless you have a breakthrough technology or innovation (with a proven market), these types of funds are difficult, if not impossible, to obtain. These types of investors typically see a massive amount of opportunities, so they have the ability to select only the best of the best businesses.

If you are considered worthy of this form of investment, you still need to be cautious due to the cost. In the majority of the situations where my clients have been offered venture capital, they have passed and found other alternatives. The reason being this type of money is typically very expensive. Expensive meaning you have to give up too much ownership (and control) of your company. If you are willing to give up control, it may make sense to simply sell your business. You get a larger amount of funds, you reduce your personal risk, and you will likely be given the opportunity to buy into the acquiring entity, essentially retaining some control.

Grants

Although grants are considered free money (you don't have to pay it back), I have seen several situations where a lot of time and money were wasted pursuing these types of funds. In the circumstances where I have seen entrepreneurs successfully obtain grant money, it has been for very specific circumstances (e.g., a mobile home reseller obtained grant money to provide mobile homes for Hurricane Katrina victims). Before you spend the time applying for specific grants, make sure you do your homework and make sure your business qualifies. Otherwise you will be wasting your time.

Vendors

Most vendors are willing to offer you some form of terms. Although you may occasionally miss out on a cash discount, vendor financing is a simple way to boost cash.

Customers

Retainers and deposits are a great interest-free way to finance your business. Although you may need to offer a discount to convince customers to comply, customer financing is a great way to boost cash flow.

Competitors

If you have strong competitors in your industry, it may make sense for you to form a strategic alliance. This joint venture can be structured in a separate entity or a simple subcontractor arrangement. Be careful! Before you approach a competitor, make sure you have the proper protections in place. I have seen numerous situations where a smaller business was pushed out of a deal because they did not take the proper precautions (e.g., non-compete agreements, non-disclosure agreements).

Market Your Financing Package

Once you have determined which financing option makes the most sense for you, it is time to take your financing package to market. I suggest you start by identifying ten to twenty potential sources in your ideal financing category (e.g., bank, private equity). Once you have created your list, you need to initiate preliminary conversations. Your goal should be to determine each lender's level of interest for providing you funding. If you are able to find three to five interested sources, you can move on to the next step. If you are having difficulty finding three to five interested sources in your ideal financing category, you need to either find additional sources in your current financing category or consider expanding your search to other categories.

Some business owners give me a hard time about finding three to five sources. Why bother if you have one source that is strongly interested? The reality is financing deals fall through constantly for a wide variety of reasons (e.g., due diligence uncovers something unexpected, underwriting won't approve the financing, your contact at the financing source is no longer there). Until you have signed the financing documents and obtained the funds, you need to keep looking for sources.

Once you have your list of three to five sources, then you need to give them your full financing package. After going through a few rounds of questions, you should be able to receive some form of formal commitment from at least one of your sources (e.g., term sheet, letter of interest). If you are unable to obtain at least one formal commitment, or if the formal commitments you are receiving are unacceptable, you need to start marketing your financing package again, meaning starting with identifying another ten to twenty potential sources from the applicable financing category.

Evaluating Financing Offers

Once you receive a number of formal commitments, it is time to select the best offer. There are a number of variables to consider, including:

1. **Availability**: The amount of actual financing available.
2. **Advance rate**: Similar to availability, the advance rate may limit your actual availability (e.g., you may have $1 million of total availability, but your advance rate limits how much of the $1 million you can actually use.) Many use a percentage of the value of one of your collateral accounts. For example, a typical advance rate against accounts receivable is 80 percent of your accounts receivable under ninety days old.
3. **Costs**: This includes interest rate(s) and fees.
4. **Structure**: The structure can be debt, equity, or a combination of the two. Debt is typically structured as a line of credit or term debt. Equity structures can include voting rights, management participation, etc.
5. **Term**: How long the financing will be available. You also need to be aware of any prepayment penalties.
6. **Covenants and restrictions**: Covenants are designed to monitor the health of the company, as well as protect the collateral. Covenants may require that your business

meet certain benchmarks (e.g., achieve a positive tangible net worth by a certain date, maintain a debt-to-equity ratio of 3-to-1). Covenants also dictate reporting requirements (e.g., quarterly financial statements, annual audit).

7. **Restrictions**: An additional type of covenant that restricts your business activities. Typical restrictions include limits on officer compensation/distribution, limits to the amount of outside financing you are able to obtain, restrictions on your company's merger/divestiture activity, etc.

I encourage you to look thoroughly at the details of your formal commitment before choosing your lender. Focusing solely on one element of the financing proposal (e.g., availability) may cause you to ignore significant negative elements of your formal commitment (e.g., overly restrictive covenants). Once you have selected the best commitment for you it is time to move on to due diligence.

Due Diligence

Most financing sources are going to perform some form of due diligence to validate your numbers. Due diligence also ensures the underlying collateral is intact and unencumbered. Due diligence may include auditing your collateral, obtaining appraisals, validating your financial statements, reviewing your tax returns, etc. This step can be both time consuming and annoying. It can also uncover issues you were unaware of (e.g., environmental problems, liens). Assuming you were forthright in your communications with the financing source, due diligence is only a formality before closing. If due diligence does uncover adverse information, the formal commitment may be offered or rescinded.

Closing

If due diligence did not uncover anything unforeseeable, the financing source will likely draft the applicable closing documents. It is critical to have a good attorney and CPA review all of the legal documents. Assuming your trusted advisors agree that the terms of the financing arrangement are consistent with the formal commitment, it is time to sign the legal paperwork and obtain your funds.

Post-Close

Whether you are dealing with a lender or investor, closing your financing deal is only the beginning of your relationship. Now that you have the funds, you need to make sure you comply with the terms and covenants of your agreement by providing reports, making the applicable payments, maintaining the agreed upon performance of the company. Failure to do so can result in law-suits, fees, increased interest rate, etc. It can also result in your business being required to pay the money back immediately.

Default

When you violate the agreed-upon terms and/or covenants of a financing arrangement, it is likely that the financial institution has the legal right to take actions against you and your business. Common violations include missing payments, violating loan cov-enants or restrictions, failure to provide agreed-upon reporting, etc. Depending on the nature of your default and your relationship with the lender, the lenders reaction may be mild (additional fees) or severe (foreclosure).

Foreclosure is the legal and professional proceeding in which a lender obtains a court-ordered termination of a lender's equitable right of redemption. Usually a lender obtains a security interest from a borrower to secure a loan. If the borrower defaults, the lender forecloses in order to take possession of the secured prop-erty, typically the collateral used in obtaining the financing.

Another possibility is restructuring your financing arrangement with your source of funds. Since the borrower is likely the only party that violated the financing arrangement, the terms of the new arrangement tend to favor the lender (e.g., additional costs, higher interest rate). The lender may also require a forbearance agreement.

Ren J. Carlton, CPA, CSMC

Forbearance is a special agreement between the lender and the borrower in order to delay a foreclosure. Loan borrowers sometimes have problems with their payments due to unexpected circumstances. This may cause the lender to start the foreclosure process. To avoid this situation, the lender and the borrower have the option to make an agreement called "forbearance." According to this agreement, the lender delays his right to exercise foreclosure if the borrower could catch-up his payment schedule in a certain amount of time. This time-period and the payment plan depend on the details of the agreement which are accepted by both of the parties involved. Wikipedia

Forbearance arrangements vary, but they almost always include frequent financial reporting and additional costs. The terms may also mandate the use of consultants, restrict the use of available funds, require the pledging of additional collateral, etc. Unless the borrower has the funds available to pay off the loans that are in default, the borrower is often at the control of the lender (since the borrower defaulted on the terms of the initial agreement).

Walking Away

Telling a business owner it is time to quit is one of the hardest parts of my job. It goes against the do-it-or-die-trying spirit of most successful entrepreneurs. The problem is sometimes walking away from a dying business is the best option. I have helped numerous clients overcome seemingly insurmountable challenges. I have also seen entrepreneurs lose everything. Before you restructure loans you have defaulted on, ask yourself some of the following questions:

1. How much will the lender accept to pay off the debt?
2. What are the terms of the restructuring/forbearance?
3. Can your business succeed under these conditions?
4. What is the worst thing that can happen if you refuse to restructure?

5. What is the worst thing that can happen if you do restructure and your business defaults again?

At some point it makes sense to stop throwing good money after bad. Outside advisors are great for offering an objective perspective, but only the stakeholder(s) can truly determine when enough is enough.

Other Alternatives

Sometimes financing is just not accessible. When that is the case, I offer two additional ideas for funding your company's operations: partnering and acquisitions.

Partnering

When your business lacks character, collateral, or capital, it may make sense to secure a strong financial partner. Financial partners come in many forms (private investor/lender, guarantor, etc.) Our clients have used friends, family, vendors, government, and even competitors to help secure financing. Make sure you consult with your trusted advisors before entering a financial partnering arrangement. I have seen businesses inadvertently given away due to cleverly drafted legal documents!

Acquisition

Buying a business? Without cash? It may seem crazy at first, but think about it. If you are hurting, what are the chances that some of your competition is hurting as well? The trick is to identify situations where 1+1=3. For example, we have structured deals where our client paid nothing out of pocket, folded the competitor into their operation, and all of the equity stakeholders made more money—including the sellers. In this circumstance, a good portion of the income benefit came from the elimination of redundant overhead (e.g., now they only needed one phone system, one computer network, etc.) The end result was a much more viable, bankable company.

Action Items

Ren J. Carlton, CPA, CSMC

1. Determine your business's financing needs
2. Identify the best source of those funds
3. Assemble a complete financing package

CHAPTER 7: FINANCIAL MANAGEMENT – BUILDING YOUR PROFIT TEAM

"Avoid the crowd. Do your own thinking independently. Be the chess player, not the chess piece." Ralph Charell

Chapter Highlights
1. Members of your financial management team
2. Roles of your financial management team
3. Options for building your profit team

Although most business owners understand the importance of having strong marketing and operational teams, the finance department is often overlooked. Just as your marketing department generates sales and your operations team produces your products/services, your finance department should drive profits. In order to create a profit-driven business, you need to have the right team in place.

Members of Your Profit Team

I will use the terms *profit team, accounting department*, and *finance department* interchangeably. Although I understand there are differences between the accounting and finance department in some businesses, these differences are not relevant to this topic. Overall both of these departments should be focused on driving profits, hence my "profit team" terminology.

Chief Financial Officer (CFO)

Your CFO is responsible for the overall financial management of your business. This role requires a mix of analytical and communication skills. True CFOs should have at least a bachelor's degree in finance or accounting, possess an MBA or CPA, have seven to ten years of finance and/or accounting experience, and have outstanding communication skills. Your CFO should have the following responsibilities:

1. Participate in strategic planning activities
2. Perform financial statement analysis
3. Prepare budgets and projections
4. Establish and maintain financing
5. Manage risk
6. Manage merger, acquisition, and divestiture activities
7. Hire, fire, train, and evaluate the controller

Participate in Strategic Planning Activities

A true CFO's role should be engaged in the overall strategic planning of the business. Strategic planning includes developing the organization's vision, formation of the core values, performing a SWOT analysis (Strengths, Weaknesses, Opportunities, Threats), setting goals for the next one to ten years, expansion/contraction planning, etc. Your CFO's role should be to contribute ideas, as well as evaluate the feasibility of the plan from a financial perspective.

Perform Financial Statement Analysis

Preparing financial statements is important, but interpreting the data is critical. Many of the techniques we described in the previous chapters assist in this function (e.g., dashboards, budget-to-actual analysis); however, it is still necessary to analyze the trends and overall condition of the company. Is the organization on track to hit the goals for the year? Are corrective actions required (e.g., downsizing, expansion, investment in equipment)? Is the available cash sufficient? These questions often can be answered through analysis of the financial statements and management reports.

Prepare Budgets and Projections

Both profitability and cash needs to be budgeted and monitored. Specific tasks include creating the annual budget, performing a monthly activity-based budget-to-actual analysis, explaining material budget variances, and recommending any applicable corrective actions. Creating projections that utilize current data to project future performance may also be needed. Additional responsibilities can include evaluating potential capital expenditures, analyzing expansion plans, etc.

Establish and Maintain Financing

This responsibility requires both analytical and interpersonal skills. This includes finding and interfacing with potential sources of funding (banks, private equity, friends/family, etc.), securing adequate financing, and maintaining relationships with financing sources. The financing function also consists of monitoring cash reserves and identifying additional sources of funding in case the need arises.

Manage Risk

On the surface, this responsibility may appear simple. The majority of organizations feel that managing risk is as simple as purchasing insurance. Although it is critical that all of the proper insurance is in place (workers' compensation, umbrella, etc.), what about the risks of entering a new market—especially outside the countries where you normally do business? Acquisitions, currency fluctuations, regulatory changes are just a sample of the risks a CFO needs to manage. Managing risk includes running the applicable what-if analysis and determining the cost-vs.-benefit of hedging the applicable risk (if possible).

One of my clients almost lost everything because of improperly managing currency fluctuation risk. In 2007, the U.S. dollar experienced a substantial weakening against the Canadian dollar. My client had numerous long-term contracts that required my client to purchase a certain product from Canada. Historically the translation adjustment was a hidden profit center (since the U.S. dollar was typically significantly stronger than the Canadian dollar). Due to the unprecedented fluctuation in currency, my client had to subsidize the currency swing. Fortunately, we were able to renegotiate terms with some of my client's customers. Although my client did suffer losses, the negative impact was manageable. It is the

CFO's job to anticipate these types of problems and make sure the business is properly protected.

Manage Merger, Acquisition, and Divestiture Activities

These types of transactions are life altering for an organization. Differences in cultures, systems, customers, product lines, and vendors can be difficult, if not impossible, to align. Failure to run the numbers and properly plan the transaction drastically increases the likelihood of disaster. Your CFO needs to manage these transactions for your organization.

I had a client that was in the process of selling their business. In the midst of negotiating terms with the buyer, news of the sale leaked to the employees. Four key operational employees stated that they were "off the table" and were going to start their own business, essentially stealing my client's customers. Fortunately we planned for this contingency. Although two of these employees did ultimately leave, they were unable to steal clients due to a non-solicitation clause in their employment agreement. Their departure did virtually no damage to the transaction or the eventual selling price of the business.

Hire, Fire, Train, and Evaluate the Controller

Since the CFO is responsible for the entire finance department, it is important to have the right team in place. The controller is responsible for providing the CFO with timely and accurate financial data, as well as building the rest of the finance team. Therefore, it is critical the CFO finds the right individual for the controller role.

Controller

Your controller is responsible for producing timely and accurate financial information. This role requires a mix of analytical and managerial skills. True controllers should have at least a bachelor's degree in finance or accounting, possess an MBA or CPA, have four to eight years of accounting experience, and have good computer skills. Your controller should have the following responsibilities:

1. Produce financial statements and management reports
2. Establish and maintain the accounting system
3. Manage cash
4. Manage costs
5. Establish and maintain internal controls
6. Hire, fire, train, and evaluate the transactional accountants

Produce Financial Statements and Management Reports

This includes performing month-end closing activities (adjusting the financial statements for accruals, prepaid assets, depreciation, etc.), producing financial statements (income statement, balance sheet, and statement of cash flows), and the applicable management reports. It is critical that these activities are produced in a timely and accurate manner.

A few years ago, we were hired by a client to evaluate their accounting department. Although this business had a full-time "CFO" and "controller" (in addition to about ten other financial people on their staff), our client was receiving financial statements at least three months late. And the late statements had errors that were identified by the owners. This caused the owners to make poor tax planning decisions in that they essentially spent money they did not have to offset income that did not exist! After building good reporting processes, we were able to help our client produce accurate financial statements by the seventh of the following month vs. three months late, an improvement of approximately eighty days.

Manage Cash

Cash is king! Although it is your CFO's job to secure financing, it is your controller's job to manage the available cash. When cash is tight, your controller needs to stretch vendor payments without disrupting the business. When cash is abundant, your controller should be taking advantage of investment opportunities (quantity discounts, cash discounts, sweep accounts, etc.).

Manage Costs

Costs need to be controlled. Budgeting is a useless exercise if the underlying expenses are not monitored. Whether it is phone service, insurance, employee benefits, or banking, it is your controller's job to periodically review costs to ensure your organization is getting the best possible price.

Establish and Maintain the Accounting System

Your controller is responsible for maintaining an adequate accounting system for your business. This includes utilizing the proper accounting software, creating job descriptions for the entire finance department, and establishing the accounting processes for the organization. This function also includes maintaining proper documentation of the entire accounting system.

Establish and Maintain Internal Controls

A good system of checks-and-balances prevents errors and fraud. Internal control activities include proper separation of duties, periodic review of subordinates' work, job rotation, mandatory vacations, etc. Although fraud happens, errors are far more frequent (e.g., double paying invoices, inaccurate invoicing). A good system of internal controls can reduce, if not eliminate, errors, as well as keep employees away from situations that invite theft/fraud.

Hire, Fire, Train, and Evaluate the Transactional Accountants

Your controller is responsible for building your financial team (except for your CFO). This team consists of the individuals that are responsible for processing the daily transactions (I refer to these people as transactional accountants). Strong transactional accountants make the production of timely and accurate financial information much simpler.

Transactional Accountants

Transactional accountants are responsible for processing your business's daily transactions. These positions typically require a lot of repetitive tasks (e.g., data entry, filing, phone calls). Transactional accountants should have a minimum of a high school degree, one to two years accounting experience, and good computer skills. Transactional accountant responsibilities include disbursements and accounts payables, invoicing and accounts receivable, payroll, job-costing, purchasing, bookkeeping, and serving as assistant to the controller or CFO.

Staffing Options

There are multiple ways to staff your profit team categorized as follows:

1. Hiring employees
2. Temporary services
3. Outsourcing

Hiring Employees

This is the most traditional method for staffing a finance department. Hiring employees has the advantage of creating long-term relationships with your business. Since employees typically stay with their employer for an extended period, your employees should have extensive knowledge of your organization and industry. You also can utilize employees to work on projects outside the scope of their job if the need arises. Hiring employees may also be your most affordable option if your business has the need for a full-time CFO, controller, and transactional accounting staff.

Hiring employees for all of your financial roles does not always make financial sense. Although transactional accountants work well in businesses with annual sales under $50 million, these size companies often have difficulty hiring a CFO and controller. Although there is a need for the CFO and controller services, it is tough to justify the costs of hiring a true CFO and controller possessing the credentials noted above.

What often happens is the business tries to improvise by hiring either a CFO or controller. This individual is often under qualified to fill one (or even both) of the roles. This individual may supplement his or her knowledge by leaning on the outside CPA for help; however, it is often a formula for disaster. Most outside CPA firms are good at accounting and tax, not at CFO and controller services (cash management, budgeting, financing, etc.)

Temporary Services

Temporary staffing companies can be a business-saving resource when crisis occurs. When one of your financial staff members disappears unexpectedly (e.g., quitting, medical condition), staffing companies can supply you with an accountant almost immediately. Although this only offers a relatively short-term solution, temporary staffing companies offer sufficient alternatives until a permanent replacement can be found.

Although the staff provided by these companies are relatively easy to hire and fire, the majority of these people are not good long-term fits for an organization. Whether it is lack of commitment, skills, or desire, people who choose to work for temp agencies are often there for a reason. If you do choose to utilize a temporary employee for a long-term assignment, it can get expensive, since you are paying both the staffing company and the employee for the work being performed.

Outsourcing

Outsourcing is used predominately to replace transactional accountants. The premise is that accounting is not one of the core functions of a business, so it should be outsourced. This allows the business to focus on its core competencies. In addition to reducing the cost of maintaining your finance department, outsourcing eliminates the human element. Essentially you are paying a vendor to complete tasks A, B, C, and D. If the outsourcing company only performs tasks A, B, and D, you can negotiate a discount, replace the vendor, etc. The situation is typically much more complicated when dealing with employees.

Although there are distinct advantages to outsourcing, there are also some drawbacks. You may lose an element of control, since frequently the work is performed off-site. You will likely have a limited amount of input regarding how the work is completed. You may also lose capacity for performing projects outside the scope of the outsourced engagement. If you are paying an outsourcing company to perform tasks A, B, C, and D, this is what you are going to get. The outsourcing company may be unable or unwilling to work on your projects (whereas employees with available time may be more than happy to help).

A relatively innovative concept is outsourcing the CFO and/or controller functions. This may be an ideal option for your businesses if you are having difficulty securing a true CFO and controller. Outsourcing allows you to get exactly the services you need, while not having the costs of employing a true CFO and/or controller. Since outsourced CFO/controller businesses typically employ a wide variety of financial specialists, this also gives you the flexibility to increase/reduce services based on your needs. Because of the flexibility and cost, outsourcing the CFO/controller function can be a viable long-term solution until the business grows to a size that warrants a full-time CFO and controller.

Indicators of Problems

It is tough to know what you don't know. How can you tell if your accounting and finance department is doing a good job? Here are some problems that indicate you need to make changes to your profit team:

1. Uninformed business decision making
2. Financial surprises

3. Ongoing cash crisis
4. Inaccurate financial reports
5. Losses
6. Lender or investor friction
7. Consistently late financial reports
8. Cash-basis financial statements
9. Turnover in accounting department

Uninformed Business Decision Making

If you think running a business is tough, try doing it blindfolded! The proper financial data is critical to making good business decisions. Whether you are buying a piece of equipment, considering expansion, or planning for taxes, you need to have a clear understanding of where your business is and where it is headed.

Financial Surprises

Good or bad financial surprises show a lack understanding and/or control in your finance department. When unplanned events occur, the financial impact of these events should be anticipated and planned for. Unpredicted swings in income and cash can have catastrophic consequences to your business. It is your financial department's job to be prepared.

Ongoing Cash Crisis

It is the CFO's job to obtain adequate financing for the operation. It is the controller's job to manage the available cash. If your organization is always dealing with a shortage of cash, it is likely one of these two areas is not being handled properly.

Inaccurate Financial Reports

I would rather receive no financial information than get inaccurate financial data. We signed a new client toward the end of the 2007 tax year. This client thought they were breaking even at best. Once we implemented our processes, we discovered they were going to make a significant profit. Good news, right? Wrong! Our client was going to pay approximately 40 percent of every dollar they earned toward taxes! And this particular client was delaying necessary capital expenditures because he thought they were performing poorly! Although we weren't able to spend as much as my client would have liked, they were able to spend down a good portion of the profit, essentially getting a 40 percent discount on everything they bought due to the tax savings.

Losses

It is the CFO and controller's job to monitor performance. If your business is losing money, your accounting department should be screaming for the applicable cost reductions (e.g., layoffs, delaying capital expenditures). Unfortunately, a lot of financial departments stop here. It is also your profit team's job to identify opportunities to become more profitable through acquisition, additional product lines, etc.

Lender or Investor Friction

It is critical your CFO keeps your funding sources happy. One of the core values of our firm is over-communication. This is definitely a formula for success with your sources of capital. Keeping your financiers informed of where you are and where you are headed is extremely important. Obviously this communication can be challenging during tough times; however, it is the CFO's job to instill confidence in your financing sources during both good and bad times.

Consistently Late Financial Reports

The older the financial data, the less useful it becomes. Timely financial information is critical to making good decisions.

Cash-Basis Financial Statements

When utilizing cash-basis statements, the financial condition of the company can be substantially different than reported. Although cash is king, accrual basis statements truly capture the revenue you have earned and the expenses you owe. Your finance department must be capable of producing accrual-based financial statements.

Turnover in Accounting Department

Frequent turnover is expensive, time-consuming, and distracting. It is your CFO and controller's job to effectively manage your accounting department. This includes identifying and retaining financial talent.

Realize that some errors and problems will occur, regardless of the strength of your accounting department. However, the indicators I outlined above should occur rarely, if ever. The greater the frequency and reoccurrence of the above problems, the greater the likelihood you need to reevaluate your profit team.

Some financial people may argue that economic factors cause some of the above problems (e.g., losses, ongoing cash crisis). I agree this is partially true; however, I would also argue that it is the CFO and controller's job to figure out how to produce profits and cash despite the economic factors. Otherwise what are you paying them for? If your sales department is not producing sales, aren't you going to hold your salespeople accountable? If this is how you run your sales department (and I hope it is), shouldn't your profit team be held accountable for the profitability of your business?

Action Items
1. Determine if all the roles of your financial management team are being filled
2. Evaluate your financial management team
3. Identify the most cost-effective method for filling all the roles on your profit team

CONCLUSION – TIME TO EXECUTE!

"When you own your own business, you only have to work half a day. You can do anything you want with the other twelve hours."
Anonymous

At time of this writing the US (and possibly the world) is in the midst of the worst economic recession in decades. While the economy will eventually recover, the world never be the same. It is unlikely that credit will ever be as readily accessible as it was throughout most of the 2000s. Global competition will continue to introduce better products and services. It will be increasingly difficult to attract and retain talent (even during double-digit national unemployment.)

Despite all of this, entrepreneurship is far from dead. Historically, several successful businesses have started during economic recessions (e.g. Microsoft, Southwest Airlines.) I have business clients that are continuing to produce outstanding financial results throughout these turbulent times. How can some entrepreneurs thrive while others struggle?

You now have the playbook for building a profit-driven business in any economic environment. If you implement our processes in your organization everyone will focus on driving profits. As far as your employees are concerned, the strong will thrive and the weak will perish.

This brings me back to the premise of this book. Is Profitpreneurship good? The techniques in this book are powerful. I guarantee you will see results if you implement our techniques properly. But our methodologies can be extremely disruptive. People will be uncomfortable. Tough decisions will need to be made. You will likely not be the most popular person in your business. Personally I have no issue with this. I'd always rather be respected than liked (I'd actually prefer both, but I will settle for respected.) It is my belief that the right kind of employees respect results. This does not mean results in spite of ethics, morality, etc. It does, however, mean that results are the focal point of the business. Whether you call it greed, Profitpreneurship, or results, it works.

Don't hesitate to contact me if you need help. I love helping fellow entrepreneurs reach their profit goals. Good luck in building your profit-driven business!

AUTHOR PROFILE

Ren J. Carlton, CPA, CSMC is a native Michigander. He graduated with honors from Oakland University and went to work for both large and small public accounting firms. With a strong desire to implement his own ideas, he moved into private industry and served as the chief financial officer for a Tier 1 manufacturing company in Troy, Michigan. Although his role as chief financial officer provided more consistent hours and a lucrative salary, Ren still felt he wasn't following his "star."

In January 2000, Ren launched Dynamic Advisory Solutions out of his basement with virtually no clients or contacts. He spent every spare minute working on DAS; planning, seeking financing, networking, and experimenting with new marketing techniques. During the early years, he supplemented his income by teaching managerial and cost accounting at Baker College, Continuing Professional Education classes to CPAs through the Michigan Association of CPAs, and entrepreneurial classes through Adult Community Education programs.

By 2005, Ren had grown Dynamic Advisory Solutions into a full-fledged management consulting firm. Once Dynamic Advisory Solutions enjoyed a nice book of clients and an outstanding staff, He revisited his teaching passion and launched his radio program. He found the excitement of pursuing "The American Dream" so much fun that he decided to share his experiences on the radio. In 2005, Ren launched The Business Reality Network radio program, a show specifically designed for aspiring entrepreneurs and established business owners. The format included business advice, business news, guests (entrepreneurs, executives, and subject-matter experts), as well as calls from the listening audience. In 2007, Ren was awarded The Michigan Small Business Journalist of the Year Award by the U.S. Small Business Administration.

Ren has participated in numerous non-profit organizations, including the Michigan Association of Certified Public Accountants

(MACPA) Ethics Task Force, the Detroit Chapter of Entrepreneur's Organization (EO) board of directors, and the Troy Community Foundation board of directors. Ren enjoys reading, learning, golf, poker, competing, teaching, and spending time with his family. Ren is energetic, passionate, and ready to share his expertise and experiences with your organization!

Visit www.rencarlton.com for more of Ren's writing, tips, and tools.

For a free phone consultation, Ren can be reached at:

(800) 440-5266
(248) 283-8834
rcarlton@daspc.com

5468640R0

Made in the USA
Charleston, SC
19 June 2010